ੴ

Understanding
The Spiritual Dialogues
Siddha Goshti

Satjit Wadva

KW

Knowledge World
KW Publisher Pvt Ltd
New Delhi

KW Publishers Pvt Ltd
4676/21, First Floor, Ansari Road, Daryaganj, New Delhi 110002
E knowledgeworld@vsnl.net **T** +91.11.23263498 / 43528107
www.kwpub.com

ISBN 978-93-83649-58-7

Published by Kalpana Shukla, KW Publishers Pvt Ltd
4676/21, First Floor, Ansari Road, Daryaganj, New Delhi 110002

2011 FPBA BEST PUBLISHERS AWARD (ENGLISH)

Typeset by Black Innovation, New Delhi
Printed and bound in India

₹ 495.00

We are born in a state of bliss. Bliss is our birth right. Everything around us is blessed. This world is dancing in ecstasy. It is continuously celebrating the never-ending festival of life. The suns, moons and stars have lit up the stage; the orchestra of trees, plants, and all the vegetation are playing the music and the rivers and mountains, birds and animals are singing the divine song. In such a blissful atmosphere, why is man in misery?

One thing is for sure that Nature did not intend to make you miserable. If you are miserable, it is your doing. If you are sad, it means you are doing something wrong. Your sorrows are not given to you; you create them yourself. What is given to you is bliss which you have forgotten completely.

All misery exists to indicate to you that somewhere you have gone wrong, you have gone off the track. Come back immediately! How? Listen to your body, listen to nature, listen to your inner being. And watch the change; look at the difference it makes; see how you become happier. The secret is: Pause! Stop running! Listen! Stop chattering!

₹ 695.00

It is said that if you want to understand the whole of Guru Granth Sahib, you can do so by understanding Japjee alone, because Guru Nanak's message was complete in Japjee itself. The rest of the Guru Granth Sahib is an interpretation, elaboration and explanation of Japjee Sahib. Japjee, the first composition of Guru Nanak, contains the most valuable and authentic expression of the divine experience he had when he went missing for three days. Japjee was his first utterance when he returned after his encounter with the divine. Japjee contains the gist of his entire journey through which he was transformed from a seeker to the enlightened master. It is a roadmap for those who wish to walk this path.

Introduction

The *Siddha Goshti* is Guru Nanak's dialogues with some sages. These sages had renounced the world and were living in caves in the Himalayas. They were yogis who believed in practising physical and mental exercises for the attainment of spiritual powers (*siddhis*), which would ultimately lead to *moksha* (liberation). These dialogues are a summary of Guru Nanak's views on life in general and spirituality in particular.

While these ascetics asserted that one must withdraw from society and family to attain detachment, Guru Nanak said that attachment and detachment were a state of mind. You don't have to give up anything; you can achieve detachment right in the middle of the marketplace. In fact, true detachment is that which can remain unruffled even in the thick of temptations. The ascetics live away from society but are dependent on the men and women of the world for their survival. Guru Nanak said that all human beings must perform their duties and fulfill their responsibilities so as not to be a burden on society.

Siddha Goshti is a series of questions and answers. The account of these meetings of Guru Nanak with the sages is recorded on pages 938 to 946 of the Guru Granth Sahib. The dialogues have been composed in and are sung in Rag Ramkali.

Siddha Goshti

ਰਾਮਕਲੀ ਮਹਲਾ ੧   ਸਿਧ ਗੋਸਟਿ   ੴ ਸਤਿਗੁਰ ਪ੍ਰਸਾਦਿ॥

ਸਿਧ ਸਭਾ ਕਰਿ ਆਸਣਿ ਬੈਠੇ ਸੰਤ ਸਭਾ ਜੈਕਾਰੋ॥
ਤਿਸੁ ਆਗੈ ਰਹਰਾਸਿ ਹਮਾਰੀ ਸਾਚਾ ਅਪਰ ਅਪਾਰੋ॥
ਮਸਤਕੁ ਕਾਟਿ ਧਰੀ ਤਿਸੁ ਆਗੈ ਤਨੁ ਮਨੁ ਆਗੈ ਦੇਉ॥
ਨਾਨਕ ਸੰਤੁ ਮਿਲੈ ਸਚੁ ਪਾਈਐ ਸਹਜ[1] ਭਾਇ ਜਸੁ ਲੇਉ॥ ੧॥

Ramkali Mahalla 1   Siddha Goshti   ੴ Satgur Prasad

Siddha sabhaa kar aasan baithey sant sabhaa jaikaaro.
Tis aagey ardaas hamari saacha apar apaaro.
Mastak kaat dha ri tis aagey tann mann aagey deo.
Nanak sant miley sach payeeye sahaj bhaaye jas leo. 1.

रामकली महला 1   सिध गोष्टि   ੴ सतगुर प्रसाद

सिध सभा कर आसण बैठे सँत सभा जैकारो।।
तिस आगे रहरास हमारी साचा अपर अपारो।।
मसतक काट धरी तिस आगे तन मन आगे देओ।।
नानक सँत मिले सच पाइए सहज भाए जस लेओ।। 1 ।।

Ramkali Mahalla 1   Siddha Goshti   ੴ Satgur Prasad

Sitting in yogic postures, forming an assembly
The Siddhas announced their presence by salutations
To the One who is true, infinite and incomparably beautiful.
Making a gesture to cut off their heads, they proclaimed
To offer their body and mind for a dialogue with him.
In response, Nanak said, "Truth showers with the Guru's blessings
And, the rest follows spontaneously."

ਕਿਆ ਭਵੀਐ ਸਚਿ ਸੂਚਾ ਹੋਇ॥
ਸਾਚ ਸਬਦ ਬਿਨੁ ਮੁਕਤਿ ਨ ਹੋਇ॥ ੧॥ ਰਹਾਉ॥
ਕਵਨ ਤੁਮੇ ਕਿਆ ਨਾਉ ਤੁਮਾਰਾ ਕਉਨੁ ਮਾਰਗੁ ਕਉਨੁ ਸੁਆਓ॥
ਸਾਚੁ ਕਹਉ ਅਰਦਾਸਿ ਹਮਾਰੀ ਹਉ ਸੰਤ ਜਨਾ ਬਲਿ ਜਾਓ॥
ਕਹ ਬੈਸਹੁ ਕਹ ਰਹੀਐ ਬਾਲੇ ਕਹ ਆਵਹੁ ਕਹ ਜਾਹੋ॥
ਨਾਨਕੁ ਬੋਲੈ ਸੁਣਿ ਬੈਰਾਗੀ ਕਿਆ ਤੁਮਾਰਾ ਰਾਹੋ॥ ੨॥

Kya bhaveeye sach soocha hoye.
Saach shabad bin mukat na hoye. 1. Rahao.
Kavan tumey kya nao tumaara kaun marag kaun suao.
Saach kaho ardaas hamari hau sant jana bal jao.
Keh baiso keh raheeye baaley keh aavo keh jaho.
Nanak boley sunn bairaagi kya tumara raho. 2.

कया भवीए सच सूचा होए।
साच सबद बिन मुकत न होए।। रहाओ ।।
कवन तुमे कया नाउ तुमारा कौन मारग कौन सुआओ।।
साच कहो अरदास हमारी हउ सन्त जना बल जाओ।।
कह बैसो कह रहीए बाले कह आवो कह जाओ।।
नानक बोले सुन बैरागी कया तुमारा राहो।। 2 ।।

"What can you achieve by wearing the attire of a yogi?
There is no salvation without the true Naam."

They asked, "Who are you? What is your name?
What is your path and your goal? Tell us where is your abode?
Where do you come from? Where are you going?
Tell us, O Nanak, what is your way?"

ਘਟਿ ਘਟਿ ਬੈਸਿ ਨਿਰੰਤਰਿ ਰਹੀਐ ਚਾਲਹਿ ਸਤਿਗੁਰ ਭਾਏ॥
ਸਹਜੇ ਆਏ ਹੁਕਮਿ ਸਿਧਾਏ ਨਾਨਕ ਸਦਾ ਰਜਾਏ॥
ਆਸਣਿ ਬੈਸਣਿ ਥਿਰੁ ਨਾਰਾਇਣੁ ਐਸੀ ਗੁਰਮਤਿ ਪਾਏ॥
ਗੁਰਮੁਖਿ ਬੂਝੈ ਆਪੁ ਪਛਾਣੈ ਸਚੇ ਸਚਿ ਸਮਾਏ॥ ੩॥

Ghat ghat bais nirantar raheeye chaaley satgur bhaaye.
Sahaje aaye hukam sidhaye Nanak sada rajaaye.
Aasan baisan thir narayan aisee gurmat paaye.
Gurmukh boojhey aap pachhaney sachey sach samaaye. 3.

घट घट बैस निरँतर रहीए चाले सतगुर भाए।।
सहजे आए हुकम सिधाए नानक सदा रजाए।।
आसण बैसण थिर नरायण ऐसी गुरमत पाए।।
गुरमुख बूझे आप पछाणे सचे सच समाए।। 3।।

Nanak said, "I live in the One that resides in every heart
I move according to the Guru's instructions following the Divine Will
I identify with the Immovable even when I am moving or am still
Gurmukh is one who knows himself and remains immersed in the Truth."

ਦੁਨੀਆ ਸਾਗਰੁ[2] ਦੁਤਰੁ ਕਹੀਐ ਕਿਉ ਕਰਿ ਪਾਈਐ ਪਾਰੋ॥
ਚਰਪਟ ਬੋਲੈ ਅਉਧੂ ਨਾਨਕ ਦੇਹੁ ਸਚਾ ਬੀਚਾਰੋ॥
ਆਪੇ ਆਖੈ ਆਪੇ ਸਮਝੈ ਤਿਸੁ ਕਿਆ ਉਤਰੁ ਦੀਜੈ॥
ਸਾਚੁ ਕਹਹੁ ਤੁਮ ਪਾਰਗਰਾਮੀ ਤੁਝੁ ਕਿਆ ਬੈਸਣੁ ਦੀਜੈ॥ ੪॥

Duniya sagar duttar kaheeye kyun kar payeeye paro.
Charpat boley audhoo Nanak deho sacha bicharo.
Aapey aakhey aapey samjhey tis kya uttar deejey.
Saach kaho tum pargrami tujh kya baisan deejey. 4.

दुनिआ सागर दुतर कहीए क्यों कर पाइए पारो।।
चरपट बोले अवधू नानक देह सचा बीचारो।।
आपे आखे आपे समझे तिस कया उतर दीजै।।
साच कहो तुम पारगरामी तुझ कया बैसण दीजै।। 4 ।।

One yogi, Charpat, asked, "The world is an ocean impossible to cross
So, tell us, O Nanak, *fakir*, your thoughts on the matter."
Nanak replied, "You have yourself said it is impossible to cross
And you have already renounced the world, so what can I say to you?"

ਜੈਸੇ ਜਲ ਮਹਿ ਕਮਲੁ ਨਿਰਾਲਮੁ ਮੁਰਗਾਈ ਨੈਸਾਣੈ॥
ਸੁਰਤਿ ਸਬਦਿ ਭਵਸਾਗਰੁ ਤਰੀਐ ਨਾਨਕ ਨਾਮ ਵਖਾਣੈ॥
ਰਹਹਿ ਇਕਾਂਤ ਏਕੋ ਮਨਿ ਵਸਿਆ ਆਸਾ ਮਾਹਿ ਨਿਰਾਸੋ॥
ਅਗਮੁ ਅਗੋਚਰੁ ਦੇਖਿ ਦਿਖਾਏ ਨਾਨਕੁ ਤਾਕਾ ਦਾਸੋ॥੫॥

Jaisey jal meh kamal niraalam murgaayee naisaaney.
Surat shabad bhavsagar tareeye Nanak naam vakhaaney.
Rahey ekaant eko mann vasya aasa maahey niraaso.
Agam agochar dekh dikhaaye Nanak taka daaso. 5.

जैसे जल मह कमल निरालम मुरगाई नैसाणै।।
सुरत सबद भवसागर तरीए नानक नाम वखाणै।।
रहै एकांत एको मन वसिआ आसा माहि निरासो।।
अगम अगोचर देख दिखाए नानक ताका दासो।। 5।।

Nanak continued, "The method is to be like the lotus
That grows in the water but remains untouched by it.
Like the duck that floats on it but does not let its wings get wet.
Likewise live in the world and remain untouched by it.
The real renunciate is one who remains silent in the din of the world,
And fixes his consciousness on the One who makes the invisible as clear as the day."

ਸੁਣਿ ਸੁਆਮੀ ਅਰਦਾਸਿ ਹਮਾਰੀ ਪੂਛਉ ਸਾਚੁ ਬੀਚਾਰੋ॥
ਰੋਸੁ ਨ ਕੀਜੈ ਉਤਰ ਦੀਜੈ ਕਿਉ ਪਾਈਐ ਗੁਰ ਦੁਆਰੋ॥
ਇਹ ਮਨੁ ਚਲਤਉ ਸਚ ਘਰਿ ਬੈਸੈ ਨਾਨਕ ਨਾਮੁ ਅਧਾਰੋ॥
ਆਪੇ ਮੇਲਿ ਮਿਲਾਏ ਕਰਤਾ ਲਾਗੈ ਸਾਚਿ ਪਿਆਰੋ॥੬॥

Sunn soami ardaas hamari poochho saach bichaaro.
Ros na keejey uttar deejey kyun payeeye gur doaaro.
Eh mann chaltau sach ghar baisey Nanak naam adhaaro.
Aapey mel milaaye karta laagey saach pyaaro. 6.

सुन सुआमी अरदास हमारी पूछो साच बीचारो।।
रोस न कीजै उतर दीजै कयों पाईए गुर दुआरो।।
इह मन चलतो सच घर बैसै नानक नाम अधारो।।
आपे मेल मिलाए करता लागै साच पिआरो।। 6।।

Question: "Listen, swami, I ask you with humility.
Don't mind and give your well-considered views
On how to find the path, the door that opens the secret."

Answer: "This fickle mind rests only when it dissolves in Naam
The union happens only when you surrender completely."

ਹਾਟੀ ਬਾਟੀ ਰਹਹਿ ਨਿਰਾਲੇ ਰੂਖਿ ਬਿਰਖਿ ਉਦਿਆਨੇ॥
ਕੰਦ ਮੂਲੁ ਅਹਾਰੋ ਖਾਈਐ ਅਉਧੂ ਬੋਲੈ ਗਿਆਨੇ॥
ਤੀਰਥਿ ਨਾਈਐ ਸੁਖੁ ਫਲੁ ਪਾਈਐ ਮੈਲੁ ਨ ਲਾਗੈ ਕਾਈ॥
ਗੋਰਖ ਪੂਤੁ ਲੋਹਾਰੀਪਾ ਬੋਲੈ ਜੋਗ ਜੁਗਤਿ ਬਿਧਿ ਸਾਈ॥ ੭॥

Haati baati rahey niraaley rukh birakh udyaaney.
Kand mool ahaaro khaayeeye audhoo boley gyaaney.
Tirath nayeeye sukh phal payeeye mael na laagey kaayee.
Gorakh poot Lohareepa boley jog jugat bidhi saayee. 7.

हाटी बाटी रहे निराले रूख बिरख उदिआने।।
कँद मूल अहारो खाईए अवधू बोले गिआने।।
तीरथ नाईए सुख फल पाईए मैल न लागै काई।।
गोरख पूत लोहारीपा बोले जोग जुगत बिधि साई।। 7।।

Question: "We are wanderers, nomads who sleep under the trees
We live on the roots, herbs and fruits of the forest.
We listen to the discourses of the learned seers.
We bathe in the holy rivers and don't allow dirt to accumulate on us."
Lohareepa, the yogi, said, "this is our method and we have reaped fruits from it."

ਹਾਟੀ ਬਾਟੀ ਨੀਦ ਨ ਆਵੈ ਪਰ ਘਰਿ ਚਿਤੁ ਨ ਡੋਲਾਈ॥
ਬਿਨੁ ਨਾਵੈ ਮਨੁ ਟੇਕੁ ਨ ਟਿਕਈ ਨਾਨਕ ਭੂਖ ਨ ਜਾਈ॥
ਹਾਟੁ ਪਟਣੁ ਘਰੁ ਗੁਰੂ ਦਿਖਾਇਆ ਸਹਜੇ ਸਚੁ ਵਾਪਾਰੋ॥
ਖੰਡਿਤ ਨਿਦ੍ਰਾ ਅਲਪ ਅਹਾਰੰ ਨਾਨਕ ਤਤੁ ਬੀਚਾਰੋ॥੮॥

Haati baati neend na aavey par ghar chit na dolaayee.
Bin naavey mann tek na tikyee Nanak bhookh na jaayee.
Haat pattan ghar gur dikhaaya sahajey sach vapaaro.
Khandit nidra alap ahaaram Nanak tatt bichaaro. 8.

हाटी बाटी नींद न आवै पर घर चित न डोलाई।।
बिन नावै मन टेक न टिकई नानक भूख न जाई।।
हाट पटण घर गुर दिखाया सहजे सच वापारो।।
खँडित निद्रा अलप अहारँ नानक तत्त बीचारो।। ८।।

Answer: "If the sleep of ignorance does not make you lose your awareness
Then it matters not where you rest – at home or in the open.
Without Naam the mind is restless and the thirst is unquenched.
With the Guru's grace I have seen the divine spark in my heart and have let go.
Meagre food and conscious sleep are the secret of right living."

ਦਰਸਨੁ ਭੇਖ ਕਰਹੁ ਜੋਗਿੰਦ੍ਰਾ ਮੁੰਦ੍ਰਾ ਝੋਲੀ ਖਿੰਥਾ॥
ਬਾਰਹ ਅੰਤਰਿ ਏਕੁ ਸਰੇਵਹੁ ਖਟੁ ਦਰਸਨ[3] ਇਕ ਪੰਥਾ॥
ਇਨ ਬਿਧਿ ਮਨੁ ਸਮਝਾਈਐ ਪੁਰਖਾ ਬਾਹੁੜਿ ਚੋਟ ਨ ਖਾਈਐ॥
ਨਾਨਕੁ ਬੋਲੈ ਗੁਰਮੁਖਿ ਬੂਝੈ ਜੋਗ ਜੁਗਤਿ ਇਵ ਪਾਈਐ॥੯॥

Darsan bhekh karo Jogindra mundra jholee khintha.
Barah antar ek sarevoh khat darsan ik pantha.
Inn bidhi mann samjhaayeeye purkha bahur chot na khaayeeye.
Nanak boley gurmukh boojhey jog jugat iv paayeeye. 9.

दरसन भेख करो जोगिन्द्रा मुन्द्रा झोली खिन्था।।
बारह अँतर एक सरेवो खट दरसन इक पन्था।।
इन बिधि मन समझाईए पुरखा बाहुड़ चोट न खाईए।।
नानक बोले गुरमुख बूझे जोग जुगत इव पाईए।। ९।।

Nanak tells Yogendra, the yogi who had raised the question,
"Wear the mantle of Naam and let your yoga be the remembrance of the One
This is the essence of the teachings of the twelve sects and six schools of philosophy.
Let your mind understand this lest you feel the pain of failure.
This method is the true yoga which will help you attain the truth."

ਅੰਤਰਿ ਸਬਦੁ ਨਿਰੰਤਰਿ ਮੁਦ੍ਰਾ ਹਉਮੈ ਮਮਤਾ ਦੂਰਿ ਕਰੀ॥
ਕਾਮੁ ਕ੍ਰੋਧੁ ਅਹੰਕਾਰੁ ਨਿਵਾਰੈ ਗੁਰ ਕੈ ਸਬਦਿ ਸੁ ਸਮਝ ਪਰੀ॥
ਖਿੰਥਾ ਝੋਲੀ ਭਰਿਪੁਰਿ ਰਹਿਆ ਨਾਨਕ ਤਾਰੈ ਏਕੁ ਹਰੀ॥
ਸਾਚਾ ਸਾਹਿਬੁ ਸਾਚੀ ਨਾਈ ਪਰਖੈ ਗੁਰ ਕੀ ਬਾਤ ਖਰੀ॥੧੦॥

Antar shabad nirantar mudra haumey mamta door kari.
Kaam krodh ahankar nivaarey gur kea shabad so samajh pari.
Khintha jholee bharpur rahya Nanak taarey ek Hari.
Saacha sahib saachi naayee parkhey gur ki baat khari.10.

अँतर सबद निरँतर मुद्रा हउमै ममता दूर करी।।
काम करोध अहँकार निवारे गुर के सबद सु समझ परी।।
खिँथा झोली भरपुर रहिआ नानक तारे एक हरी।।
साचा साहिब साची नाई परखे गुर की बात खरी।।10।।

"The method is to let Naam reside in your heart continuously
And remove ego and attachment from it.
Shed lust, anger, ego and make room for the Guru's word.
Wear the mantle of Naam which is the only saviour
Come and see for yourself the one and only master."

ਉਧੰਉ ਖਪਰੁ ਪੰਚ ਭੂ ਟੋਪੀ[4]॥
ਕਾਂਇਆ ਕੜਾਸਣੁ ਮਨੁ ਜਾਗੋਟੀ॥
ਸਤੁ ਸੰਤੋਖੁ ਸੰਜਮੁ ਹੈ ਨਾਲਿ॥
ਨਾਨਕ ਗੁਰਮੁਖਿ ਨਾਮੁ ਸਮਾਲਿ॥੧੧॥

Undho khappar punch bhoo topi.
Kaya karhaasan mann jagoti.
Sat santokh sanjam hai naal.
Nanak gurmukh naam samaal. 11.

ऊँधो खपर पँच भू टोपी।।
काया कड़ासण मन जागोटी।।
सत सँतोख सँजम है नाल।।
नानक गुरमुख नाम समाल।। 11।।

"Let detachment from the worldly pleasures be your begging bowl
Let the divine attributes of the five elements be your cap
Let the body be your prayer mat and the mind your loin cloth
Let truth, contentment and discipline be your companions."
Nanak says, "Let this be your method of meditation."

ਕਵਨੁ ਸੁ ਗੁਪਤਾ ਕਵਨੁ ਸੁ ਮੁਕਤਾ॥
ਕਵਨੁ ਸੁ ਅੰਤਰਿ ਬਾਹਰਿ ਜੁਗਤਾ॥
ਕਵਨੁ ਸੁ ਆਵੈ ਕਵਨੁ ਸੁ ਜਾਇ॥
ਕਵਨੁ ਸੁ ਤ੍ਰਿਭਵਣਿ ਰਹਿਆ ਸਮਾਇ॥੧੨॥

Kavan so gupta kavan so mukta.
Kavan so antar bahar jugta.
Kavan so aavey kavan so jaaye.
Kavan so tribhavan rahya samaaye. 12.

कवन सु गुपता कवन सु जुगता।।
कवन सु अँतर बाहर जुगता।।
कवन सु आवै कवन सु जाए।।
कवन सु त्रिभवन रहिआ समाए।। 12।।

Question: "Who is hidden? Who is free?
Who is united inside and outside?
Who comes and who goes?
Who is that which permeates the three worlds?"

ਘਟਿ ਘਟਿ ਗੁਪਤਾ ਗੁਰਮੁਖਿ ਮੁਕਤਾ॥
ਅੰਤਰਿ ਬਾਹਰਿ ਸਬਦਿ ਸੁ ਜੁਗਤਾ॥
ਮਨਮੁਖਿ ਬਿਨਸੈ ਆਵੈ ਜਾਇ॥
ਨਾਨਕ ਗੁਰਮੁਖਿ ਸਾਚਿ ਸਮਾਇ॥੧੩॥

Ghat ghat gupta gurmukh mukta.
Antar bahar shabad so jugta.
Manmukh binsey aavey jaaye.
Nanak gurmukh saach samaaye. 13.

घट घट गुपता गुरमुख[6] मुकता।।
अँतर बाहर सबद सु जुगता।।
मनमुख बिनसै आवै जाए।।
नानक गुरमुख साच समाए।। 13।।

Answer: "The one and only Creator lives in every heart
The *gurmukh* is free and is united with the Creator inside out,
The *manmukh* comes and goes and is destroyed
While the *gurmukh* remains immersed in the Divine always."

ਕਿਉ ਕਰਿ ਬਾਧਾ ਸਰਪਨਿ ਖਾਧਾ॥
ਕਿਉ ਕਰਿ ਖੋਇਆ ਕਿਉ ਕਰਿ ਲਾਧਾ॥
ਕਿਉ ਕਰਿ ਨਿਰਮਲੁ ਕਿਉ ਕਰਿ ਅੰਧਿਆਰਾ॥
ਇਹੁ ਤਤੁ ਬਿਚਾਰੈ ਸੁ ਗੁਰੂ ਹਮਾਰਾ॥੧੪॥

Kyun kar baadha sarpan khaadha.
Kyun kar khoya kyun kar laadha.
Kyun kar nirmal kyun kar andhiyaara.
Eh tatt bichaarey so guru hamara. 14.

क्यों कर बाधा सरपन खाधा।।
क्यों कर खोया क्यों कर लाधा।।
क्यों कर निरमल क्यों कर अँधिआरा।।
इह तत बिचारे सु गुरू हमारा।। 14।।

Question: "How is man in bondage?
How is he consumed by the serpent of maya?
How has he lost himself? How will he find himself?
How has he landed himself in the darkness of ignorance?
How can he become light and pure?
Whoever gives us this wisdom is our Guru."

ਦੁਰਮਤਿ ਬਾਧਾ ਸਰਪਨਿ ਖਾਧਾ॥
ਮਨਮੁਖਿ ਖੋਇਆ ਗੁਰਮੁਖਿ ਲਾਧਾ॥
ਸਤਿਗੁਰੁ ਮਿਲੈ ਅੰਧੇਰਾ ਜਾਇ॥
ਨਾਨਕ ਹਉਮੈ ਮੇਟਿ ਸਮਾਇ॥੧੫॥

Durmat baadha sarpan khaadha.
Manmukh khoya gurmukh laadha.
Satguru miley andhera jaaye.
Nanak haumei maet samaaye. 15.

दुरमत बाधा सरपन खाधा।।
मनमुख खोया गुरमुख लाधा।।
सतगुर मिले अँधेरा जाए।।
नानक हउमै मेट समाए।। 15।।

Answer: "Man is bound by his ego.
He is consumed by his insatiable desires.
Led by his wanton mind he will remain lost forever.
Following the Guru's advice will pull him out of darkness.
Meeting with the Guru will dispel all darkness.
Breaking the wall of ego he becomes one with the Creator."

ਸੁੰਨ ਨਿਰੰਤਰਿ ਦੀਜੈ ਬੰਧ॥
ਉਡੈ ਨ ਹੰਸਾ ਪੜੈ ਨ ਕੰਧ॥
ਸਹਜ ਗੁਫਾ ਘਰੁ ਜਾਣੈ ਸਾਚਾ॥
ਨਾਨਕ ਸਾਚੇ ਭਾਵੈ ਸਾਚਾ॥੧੬॥

Sunn nirantar deejey bandh.
Uddey na hansa parhey na kandh.
Sahaj gufa ghar jaaney saacha.
Nanak saachey bhaavey saacha. 16.

सुँन निरँतर दीजै बँध।।
उडै न हँसा पड़ै न कँध।।
सहज गुफा धर जाणे साचा।।
नानक साचे भावे साचा।। 16।।

Answer continued: "Silencing the mind he attains the state of *shunya*
Where the mind stops wandering and the body remains intact
Then he resides in the cave of *sahaj* or existence as it is
Spontaneously accepting life as it unfolds naturally.
Such is the final or fourth state of being when the drop falls in the ocean."

ਕਿਸੁ ਕਾਰਣਿ ਗ੍ਰਿਹੁ ਤਜਿਓ ਉਦਾਸੀ॥
ਕਿਸੁ ਕਾਰਣਿ ਇਹੁ ਭੇਖੁ ਨਿਵਾਸੀ॥
ਕਿਸੁ ਵਖਰ ਕੇ ਤੁਮ ਵਣਜਾਰੇ॥
ਕਿਉ ਕਰਿ ਸਾਥੁ ਲੰਘਾਵਹੁ ਪਾਰੇ॥੧੭॥

Kis kaaran greh tajeyo Udaasi.
Kis kaaran eh bhekh nivaasi.
Kis vakhkhar ke tum vanjaarey.
Kyun kar saach langhaavoh paarey. 17.

किस कारण गृह तजियो उदासी।।
किस कारण इह भेख निवासी।।
किस वखर के तुम वणजारे।।
क्यों कर साथ लँघावो पारे।। 17।।

Question: "Why have you renounced your home?
Why are you roaming like a wanderer?
Why have you adopted this religious attire?
What is the commodity that you trade in?
How will you ferry others across?"

ਗੁਰਮੁਖਿ ਖੋਜਤ ਭਏ ਉਦਾਸੀ॥
ਦਰਸਨ ਕੈ ਤਾਈ ਭੇਖ ਨਿਵਾਸੀ॥
ਸਾਚ ਵਖਰ ਕੇ ਹਮ ਵਣਜਾਰੇ॥
ਨਾਨਕ ਗੁਰਮੁਖਿ ਉਤਰਸਿ ਪਾਰੇ॥੧੮॥

Gurmukh khojat bhaye udaasi.
Darsan kae taayee bhekh niwaasi.
Saach vakhkhar ke hum vanjaarey.
Nanak gurmukh utaras paarey. 18.

गुरमुख खोजत भए उदासी।।
दरसन कै ताई भेख निवासी।।
साच वखर के हम वणजारे।।
नानक गुरमुख उतरस पारे।। 18।।

Answer: "I have left home in search of a *gurmukh*.
The attire I have adopted is for easy recognition
The one and only commodity I trade in is Truth
Those who listen to the Guru will be ferried across effortlessly."

ਕਿਤੁ ਬਿਧਿ ਪੁਰਖਾ ਜਨਮੁ ਵਟਾਇਆ॥
ਕਾਹੇ ਕਉ ਤੁਝੁ ਇਹੁ ਮਨੁ ਲਾਇਆ॥
ਕਿਤੁ ਬਿਧਿ ਆਸਾ ਮਨਸਾ ਖਾਈ॥
ਕਿਤੁ ਬਿਧਿ ਜੋਤਿ ਨਿਰੰਤਰਿ ਪਾਈ॥
ਬਿਨੁ ਦੰਤਾ ਕਿਉ ਖਾਈਐ ਸਾਰੁ॥
ਨਾਨਕ ਸਾਚਾ ਕਰਹੁ ਬੀਚਾਰੁ॥੧੯॥

Kit bidhi purkha janam vataaya.
Kahey ko tujh eh mann laaya.
Kit bidhi aasa mansa khaayee.
Kit bidhi jot nirantar payee.
Bin danta kyun khaayeeye saar.
Nanak saacha karo bichaar. 19.

कित बिधि पुरखा जनम वटाया।।
काहे को तुझ इह मन लाया।।
कित बिधि आसा मनसा खाई।।
कित बिधि जोत निरँतर पाई।।
बिन दँतां क्यों खाईए सार।।
नानक साचा करो बीचार।। 19।।

Question: "How have you transformed your life?
What have you attuned your mind to?
How have you diminished your hopes and desires?
How have you hit upon the Eternal Light?
How have you done this which is like chewing iron without teeth?
Tell us, O Nanak, how have you come to this state of being?"

ਸਤਿਗੁਰ ਕੈ ਜਨਮੇ ਗਵਨੁ ਮਿਟਾਇਆ॥
ਅਨਹਤਿ ਰਾਤੇ ਇਹੁ ਮਨੁ ਲਾਇਆ॥
ਮਨਸਾ ਆਸਾ ਸਬਦਿ ਜਲਾਈ॥
ਗੁਰਮੁਖਿ ਜੋਤਿ ਨਿਰੰਤਰਿ ਪਾਈ॥
ਤ੍ਰੈ ਗੁਣ ਮੇਟੇ ਖਾਈਐ ਸਾਰੁ॥
ਨਾਨਕ ਤਾਰੇ ਤਾਰਣਹਾਰੁ॥ ੨੦॥

Satgur ke janamey gavan mitaaya.
Anhat raatey eh mann laaya.
Mansa aasa shabad jalaayee.
Gurmukh jot nirantar payee.
Trai gunn metey khaayeeye saar.
Nanak taarey taaranhaar. 20.

सतगुर कै जनमे गवन मिटाया।।
अनहत राते इह मन लाया।।
मनसा आसा सबद जलाई।।
गुरमुख जोत निरँतर पाई।।
त्रै गुण मेटे खाईए सार।।
नानक तारे तारणहार।। 20।।

Answer: "With the grace of the Guru,
I am liberated from the cycle of birth and death.
My mind is attuned to the unstruck sound of *Omkar.*
The sound of Naam has dispelled my hopes and desires.
And the eternal light illuminates my heart.
Getting past the three states of being I have attained the fourth
Which is, as you say, like eating iron without teeth."

ਆਦਿ ਕਉ ਕਵਨੁ ਬੀਚਾਰੁ ਕਥੀਅਲੇ ਸੁੰਨ ਕਹਾ ਘਰ ਵਾਸੋ॥
ਗਿਆਨ ਕੀ ਮੁਦ੍ਰਾ ਕਵਨ ਕਥੀਅਲੇ ਘਟਿ ਘਟਿ ਕਵਨ ਨਿਵਾਸੋ॥
ਕਾਲ ਕਾ ਠੀਗਾ ਕਿਉ ਜਲਾਈਅਲੇ ਕਿਉ ਨਿਰਭਉ ਘਰਿ ਜਾਈਐ॥
ਸਹਜ ਸੰਤੋਖ ਕਾ ਆਸਣੁ ਜਾਣੈ ਕਿਉ ਛੇਦੇ ਬੈਰਾਈਐ॥
ਗੁਰ ਕੈ ਸਬਦਿ ਹਉਮੈ ਬਿਖੁ ਮਾਰੈ ਤਾ ਨਿਜ ਘਰਿ ਹੋਵੈ ਵਾਸੋ॥
ਜਿਨਿ ਰਚਿ ਰਚਿਆ ਤਿਸੁ ਸਬਦਿ ਪਛਾਣੈ ਨਾਨਕੁ ਤਾ ਕਾ ਦਾਸੋ॥੨੧॥

Aad ko kavan bichaar kathialey sunn kaha ghar vaaso.
Gyan ki mudra kavan kathialey ghat ghat kavan nivaaso.
Kaal ka theega kyun jalaayeeley kyun nibhau ghar jayeeye.
Sahaj santokh ka aasan jaaney kyun chhedey bairaayeeye.
Gur kae shabad haumei bikh maarey ta nij ghar hovey vaaso.
Jin rach rachya tis shabad pachhaaney Nanak ta ka daaso. 21.

आद को कवन बीचार कथीअले सुँन कहा घर वासो।।
गिआन की मुद्रा कवन कथीअले घट घट कवन निवासो।।
काल का ठीगा क्यों जलाईए क्यों निरभउ घर जाईए।।
सहज सँतोख का आसण जाणे क्यों छेदे बैराईए।।
गुर कै सबद हउमै बिख मारे ता निज घर होवे वासो।।
जिन रच रचिआ तिस सबद पछाणे नानक ता का दासो।। 21।।

Question: "What was the state of existence before the creation?
Where in your opinion did the Creator reside before the creation?
What were the mudras or methods of acquiring knowledge?
Who was residing in every heart then? How can we avert the blow of death?
How can we achieve the state of fearlessness? How can we conquer our foes?"

Answer: "In the backdrop of *sahaj* and contentment
Kill the poison of ego with the Guru's word
Then only you can remain grounded in your home (self)
I surrender myself to the Creator who has revealed the secret through Naam."

ਕਹਾ ਤੇ ਆਵੈ ਕਹਾ ਇਹੁ ਜਾਵੈ ਕਹਾ ਇਹੁ ਰਹੈ ਸਮਾਈ॥
ਏਸੁ ਸਬਦ ਕਉ ਜੋ ਅਰਥਾਵੈ ਤਿਸੁ ਗੁਰ ਤਿਲੁ ਨ ਤਮਾਈ॥
ਕਿਉ ਤਤੈ ਅਵਿਗਤੈ ਪਾਵੈ ਗੁਰਮੁਖਿ ਲਗੈ ਪਿਆਰੋ॥
ਆਪੇ ਸੁਰਤਾ ਆਪੇ ਕਰਤਾ ਕਹੁ ਨਾਨਕ ਬੀਚਾਰੋ॥
ਹੁਕਮੇ ਆਵੈ ਹੁਕਮੇ ਜਾਵੈ ਹੁਕਮੇ ਰਹਿਆ ਸਮਾਈ॥
ਪੂਰੇ ਗੁਰ ਤੇ ਸਾਚੁ ਕਮਾਵੈ ਗਤਿ ਮਿਤਿ ਸਬਦੇ ਪਾਈ॥੨੨॥

Kaha te aavey kaha eh javey kaha eh rahya samaayee.
Eas shabad ko jo arthavey tis gur til na tamaayee.
Kyun tattey avigatay paavey gurmukh lagey pyaaro.
Aapey surta aapey karta kaho Nanak bichaaro.
Hukmey aavey hukmey jaavey hukmey rahya samaayee.
Poorey gur te saach kamaavey gatt mitt shabadey payee. 22.

कहा ते आवे कहा इह जावे कहा इह रहै समाई।।
एस सबद को जो अरथावे तिस गुर तिल न तमाई।।
क्यों ततै अविगतै पावे गुरमुख लगै पिआरो।।
आपे सुरता आपे करता कहो नानक बीचारो।।
हुकमे आवे हुकमे जावे हुकमे रहिआ समाई।।
पूरे गुर ते साच कमावे गत मित सबदे पाई।। 23।।

Question: "Where from does it come and whereto it goes and where does it remain?
Whoever tells us this secret is the true guru, devoid of any vices.
How can the creature find its source who is both the Creator and the creation?"
Nanak says: "Creativity includes everything–the Creator and the creation.
His *hukam* is the prime mover which makes things come and go and remain constant.
The true guru imparts this knowledge and realisation comes through Naam."

ਆਦਿ ਕਉ ਬਿਸਮਾਦੁ ਕਥੀਅਲੇ ਸੁੰਨ ਨਿਰੰਤਰਿ ਵਾਸੁ ਲੀਆ॥
ਅਕਲਪਤ ਮੁਦ੍ਰਾ ਗੁਰ ਗਿਆਨੁ ਬੀਚਾਰੀਅਲੇ ਘਟਿ ਘਟਿ ਸਾਚਾ ਸਰਬ ਜੀਆ॥
ਗੁਰ ਬਚਨੀ ਅਵਿਗਤਿ ਸਮਾਈਐ ਤਤੁ ਨਿਰੰਜਨੁ ਸਹਜਿ ਲਹੈ॥
ਨਾਨਕ ਦੂਜੀ ਕਾਰ ਨ ਕਰਣੀ ਸੇਵੈ ਸਿਖੁ ਸੁ ਖੋਜਿ ਲਹੈ॥
ਹੁਕਮੁ ਬਿਸਮਾਦੁ ਹੁਕਮਿ ਪਛਾਣੈ ਜੀਅ ਜੁਗਤਿ ਸਚੁ ਜਾਣੈ ਸੋਈ॥
ਆਪੁ ਮੇਟਿ ਨਿਰਾਲਮੁ ਹੋਵੈ ਅੰਤਰਿ ਸਾਚੁ ਜੋਗੀ ਕਹੀਐ ਸੋਈ॥੨੩॥

Aad ko bismaad kathialey sunn nirantar vaas liya.
Akalpat mudra gur gyan bichaariley ghat ghat saacha sarab jiya.
Gur bachni avigatt samayeeye tatt niranjan sahaj lahey.
Nanak duji kaar na karni sevey sikh su khoj lahey.
Hukam bismaad hukam pachhaney jee jugat sach jaaney soyee.
Aap maet niralam hovey antar saach jogi kaheeye soyee. 23.

आद को बिसमाद कथीअले सुँन निरँतर वास लीआ।।
अकलपत मुद्रा गुर गिआन बीचारीअले घट घट साचा सरब जीआ।।
गुर बचनी अविगत समाईऐ तत निरँजन सहज लहै।।
नानक दूजी कार न करणी सेवे सिख सो खोज लहै।।
हुकम बिसमाद हुकमे पछाणे जीअ जुगत सच जाणे सोई।।
आप मेट निरालम होवे अँतर साच जोगी कहीए सोई।। 24।।

Answer: "We can only wonder at the beginning when the Creator rested in *shunya.*
Let desirelessness be the posture to realise the One that resides in every heart.
Remain attuned to the Guru's word and you will attain the formless deity.
There is no need to do anything else if you can follow the Guru's advice.
The secret of life is revealed when you live in accordance with the *hukam.*
Destroy the ego, remain detached, and look within to become a true yogi."

ਅਵਿਗਤੋ ਨਿਰਮਾਇਲੁ ਉਪਜੇ ਨਿਰਗੁਣ ਤੇ ਸਰਗੁਣ ਥੀਆ॥
ਸਤਿਗੁਰ ਪਰਚੈ ਪਰਮ ਪਦੁ ਪਾਈਐ ਸਾਚੈ ਸਬਦਿ ਸਮਾਇ ਲੀਆ॥
ਏਕੇ ਕਉ ਸਚੁ ਏਕਾ ਜਾਣੈ ਹਉਮੈ ਦੂਜਾ ਦੂਰਿ ਕੀਆ॥
ਸੋ ਜੋਗੀ ਗੁਰ ਸਬਦੁ ਪਛਾਣੈ ਅੰਤਰਿ ਕਮਲੁ ਪ੍ਰਗਾਸੁ ਥੀਆ॥
ਜੀਵਤੁ ਮਰੈ ਤਾ ਸਭੁ ਕਿਛੁ ਸੂਝੈ ਅੰਤਰਿ ਜਾਣੈ ਸਰਬ ਦਇਆ॥
ਨਾਨਕ ਤਾ ਕਉ ਮਿਲੈ ਵਡਾਈ ਆਪੁ ਪਛਾਣੈ ਸਰਬ ਜੀਆ॥੨੪॥

Avigato nirmayal upajey nirgunn te sargunn theeya.
Satgur parchey param padd paayeeye saachey shabad samaye leeya.
Ekey ko sach eka jaaney haumei duja door keeya.
So jogi gur shabad pachhaney antar kamal pragaas theeya.
Jeevat marey ta sabh kichh soojey antar jaaney sarab daya.
Nanak ta ko miley vadaayee aap pachhaney sarab jeeya. 24.

अविगतो निरमायल उपजे निरगुण ते सरगुण थीआ।।
सतगुर परचै परम पद पाईए साचै सबद समाए लीआ।।
एके को सच एका जाणै हउमै दूजा दूर कीआ।।
सो जोगी गुर सबद पछाणै अँतर कमल प्रगास थीआ।।
जीवत मरै ता सभ किछ सूजै अँतर जाणै सरब दया।।
नानक ता को मिलै वडाई आप पछाणै सरब जीआ।। 24।।

"From the formless came the innumerable forms in which He resides continuously.
With the Guru's blessings we can come to this realisation through Naam.
And we become capable of seeing the One in everything, dispelling all dualities caused by the ego.
Such is the true yogi who is enlightened by the Guru's grace
He is the living dead who knows all and is deeply compassionate.
He is truly praiseworthy who sees himself (the same light) in every being.

ਸਾਚੋ ਉਪਜੈ ਸਾਚਿ ਸਮਾਵੈ ਸਾਚੇ ਸੂਚੇ ਏਕ ਮਇਆ॥
ਝੂਠੇ ਆਵਹਿ ਠਵਰ ਨ ਪਾਵਹਿ ਦੂਜੈ ਆਵਾ ਗਉਣ ਭਇਆ॥
ਆਵਾ ਗਉਣ ਮਿਟੈ ਗੁਰ ਸਬਦੀ ਆਪੇ ਪਰਖੈ ਬਖਸਿ ਲਇਆ॥
ਏਕਾ ਬੇਦਨ ਦੂਜੈ ਬਿਆਪੀ ਨਾਮੁ ਰਸਾਇਣੁ ਵੀਸਰਿਆ॥
ਸੋ ਬੂਝੈ ਜਿਸੁ ਆਪਿ ਬੁਝਾਏ ਗੁਰ ਕੈ ਸਬਦਿ ਸੁ ਮੁਕਤੁ ਭਇਆ॥
ਨਾਨਕ ਤਾਰੇ ਤਾਰਣਹਾਰਾ ਹਉਮੈ ਦੂਜਾ ਪਰਹਰਿਆ॥੨੫॥

Saacho upajey saach samaavey saachey suchey ek mayaa.
Jhoothey aavey thavar na paavey dujey aava gavan bhayaa.
Aava gavan mitey gur shabadi aapey parkhey bakhas layaa.
Eka bedan dujey biyaapi naam rasayan viisarya.
So bujhey jis aap bujhaaye gur ke shabad so mukat bhayaa.
Nanak taarey taaranhara haumei duja parharyaa. 25.

साचो उपजै साच समावै साचे सूचे एक मया।।
झूठे आवे ठवर न पावे दूजै आवा गौण भया।।
आवा गौण मिटे गुर सबदी आपे परखे बखस लया।।
एका बेदन दूजै बिआपी नाम रसायण वीसरिआ।।
सो बूझे जिस आप बुझाए गुर कै सबद सु मुकत भया।।
नानक तारे तारणहारा हउमै दूजा परहरिआ।।

Born out of truth, sustained in truth, we can remain one with the True One
But, we identify with the false and are caught in the cycle of birth and death.
This cycle can be broken with the benevolent Guru's word.
We suffer from only one ailment–identifying with the other and forgetting the True Naam
Only he can see this clearly and be liberated who is blessed by the Guru
The benevolent Lord will help you ferry across if you remove the ego out of the way.

ਮਨਮੁਖਿ ਭੂਲੈ ਜਮ ਕੀ ਕਾਣਿ॥
ਪਰ ਘਰੁ ਜੋਹੈ ਹਾਣੈ ਹਾਣਿ॥
ਮਨਮੁਖਿ ਭਰਮਿ ਭਵੈ ਬੇਬਾਣਿ॥
ਵੇਮਾਰਗਿ ਮੂਸੈ ਮੰਤ੍ਰਿ ਮਸਾਣਿ॥
ਸਬਦੁ ਨ ਚੀਨੈ ਲਵੈ ਕੁਬਾਣਿ॥
ਨਾਨਕ ਸਾਚਿ ਰਤੇ ਸੁਖੁ ਜਾਣਿ॥੨੬॥

Manmukh bhooley jamm ki kaan.
Par ghar johey haaney haan.
Manmukh bharam bhavey bebaan.
Vemarag moosey mantar masaan.
Shabad na cheeney lavey kubaan.
Nanak saach ratey sukh jaan. 26.

मनमुख भूलै जम की काण।।
पर घर जोहै हाणै हाण।।
मनमुख भरमे भवै बेबाण।।
वेमारग मूसै मँत्र मसाण।।
सबद न चीनै लवै कुबाण।।
नानक साच रते सुख जाण।। 26।।

Manmukh has gone astray and is a slave of death
He is in the service of the false, an unsound investment bound to fail.
He goes round and round in circles and lands in bewilderment.
He is like the yogi chanting mantras in the cemetry liable to be robbed.
He knows not the Naam and talks incoherently.
Whereas it is so easy to follow the Guru's word and rejoice.

ਗੁਰਮੁਖਿ ਸਾਚੇ ਕਾ ਭਉ ਪਾਵੈ॥
ਗੁਰਮੁਖਿ ਬਾਣੀ ਅਘੜੁ ਘੜਾਵੈ॥
ਗੁਰਮੁਖਿ ਨਿਰਮਲ ਹਰਿ ਗੁਣ ਗਾਵੈ॥
ਗੁਰਮੁਖਿ ਪਵਿਤ੍ਰ ਪਰਮ ਪਦੁ ਪਾਵੈ॥
ਗੁਰਮੁਖਿ ਰੋਮਿ ਰੋਮਿ ਹਰਿ ਧਿਆਵੈ॥
ਨਾਨਕ ਗੁਰਮੁਖਿ ਸਾਚਿ ਸਮਾਵੈ॥੨੭॥

Gurmukh saachey ka bhau paavey.
Gurmukh baani agharh ghahraavey.
Gurmukh nirmal hari gunn gaavey.
Gurmukh pavitar param padd paavey.
Gurmukh rom rom Hari dhiaavey.
Nanak gurmukh saach samaavey. 27.

गुरमुख साचे का भउ पावै।।
गुरमुख बाणी अघड़ घड़ावै।।
गुरमुख निरमल हरि गुण गावै।।
गुरमुख पवित्र परम पद पावै।।
गुरमुख रोम रोम हरि धिआवै।।
नानक गुरमुख साच समावै।। 27।।

Gurmukh is the one who listens to the Guru's word and follows it.
He tightens his grip on the wanton mind with the help of the Guru.
He reads, learns and follows the Guru's advice.
He unclutters his mind and sharpens his senses to realise His presence within
He remembers the Divine with each and every fibre of his body
Thus he becomes one with the Divine like the drop unites with the ocean.

ਗੁਰਮੁਖਿ ਪਰਚੈ ਬੇਦ ਬੀਚਾਰੀ॥
ਗੁਰਮੁਖਿ ਪਰਚੈ ਤਰੀਐ ਤਾਰੀ॥
ਗੁਰਮੁਖਿ ਪਰਚੈ ਸੁ ਸਬਦਿ ਗਿਆਨੀ॥
ਗੁਰਮੁਖਿ ਪਰਚੈ ਅੰਤਰਿ ਬਿਧਿ ਜਾਨੀ॥
ਗੁਰਮੁਖਿ ਪਾਈਐ ਅਲਖ ਅਪਾਰੁ॥
ਨਾਨਕ ਗੁਰਮੁਖਿ ਮੁਕਤਿ ਦੁਆਰੁ॥੨੮॥

Gurmukh parchey ved bichaaree.
Gurmukh parchey tareeye taaree.
Gurmukh parchey so shabad gyaanee.
Gurmukh parchey antar bidhi jaanee.
Gurmukh paayeeye alakh apaar.
Nanak gurmukh mukat duaar. 28.

गुरमुख परचै बेद बीचारी।।
गुरमुख परचै तरीए तारी।।
गुरमुख परचै सु सबद गिआनी।।
गुरमुख परचै अँतर बिधि जानी।।
गुरमुख पाईए अलख अपार।।
नानक गुरमुख मुकत दुआर।। 28।।

Pleased by the *gurmukh* the Guru grants him knowledge of the Vedas
Pleased by the *gurmukh* the Guru ferries him across the ocean of desire
Pleased by the *gurmukh* the Guru reveals to him the secret of Naam
Pleased by the *gurmukh* the Guru leads him on to the inner journey.
The *gurmukh* attains to the invisible and the infinite.
Thus the *gurmukh* finds the door of liberation.

ਗੁਰਮੁਖਿ ਅਕਥ ਕਥੈ ਬੀਚਾਰਿ॥

ਗੁਰਮੁਖਿ ਨਿਬਹੈ ਸਪਰਵਾਰਿ॥

ਗੁਰਮੁਖਿ ਜਪੀਐ ਅੰਤਰਿ ਪਿਆਰਿ॥

ਗੁਰਮੁਖਿ ਪਾਈਐ ਸਬਦਿ ਅਚਾਰਿ॥

ਸਬਦਿ ਭੇਦਿ ਜਾਣੈ ਜਾਣਾਈ॥

ਨਾਨਕ ਹਉਮੈ ਜਾਲਿ ਸਮਾਈ॥੨੯॥

Gurmukh akath kathey bichaar.

Gurmukh nibahay saparvaar.

Gurmukh japeeye antar pyaar.

Gurmukh paayeeye shabad achaar.

Shabad bhed jaaney janaayee.

Nanak haumei jaal samaayee. 29.

गुरमुख अकथ कथै बीचार।।
गुरमुख निबहै सपरवार।।
गुरमुख जपीऐ अँतर प्यार।।
गुरमुख पाईए सबद अचार।।
सबद भेद जाणे जाणाई।।
नानक हउमै जाल समाई।। 29।।

The *gurmukh* contemplates and expresses that which cannot be articulated
The *gurmukh* lives a spiritually evolving life in the midst of his family.
The *gurmukh* remembers the Divine lovingly.
The *gurmukh* patterns his life according to the Divine Will.
The *gurmukh* finds the secret of Naam and helps others to see it too.
The *gurmukh* burns his ego and becomes one with the Divine.

ਗੁਰਮੁਖਿ ਧਰਤੀ ਸਾਚੈ ਸਾਜੀ॥
ਤਿਸ ਮਹਿ ਓਪਤਿ ਖਪਤਿ ਸੁ ਬਾਜੀ॥
ਗੁਰ ਕੈ ਸਬਦਿ ਰਪੈ ਰੰਗ ਲਾਇ॥
ਸਾਚਿ ਰਤਉ ਪਤਿ ਸਿਉ ਘਰਿ ਜਾਇ॥
ਸਾਚ ਸਬਦ ਬਿਨੁ ਪਤਿ ਨਹੀ ਪਾਵੈ॥
ਨਾਨਕ ਬਿਨੁ ਨਾਵੈ ਕਿਉ ਸਾਚਿ ਸਮਾਵੈ॥ ੩੦॥

Gurmukh dharti saachey saajee.
Tis meh opat khapat su baajee.
Gur ke shabad rapay rang laaye.
Saach ratto patt seo ghar jaaye.
Saach shabad bin patt nahi paavey.
Nanak bin naavey kyun saach samaavey. 30.

गुरमुख धरती साचै साजी।।
तिस मह ओपत खपत सु बाजी।।
गुर कै सबद रपै रँग लाए।।
साच रतो पत सिउ घर जाए।।
साच सबद बिन पत नहीं पावै।।
नानक बिन नावै क्यों साच समावै।। 30।।

The Creator made the world primarily for the *gurmukhs*
And in that world other creatures come and go.
The *gurmukh* remains imbued in the hues of Naam.
Dyed in colours of love the *gurmukh* returns home honourably.
Without the true Naam there is no honour.
Without Naam how can he become one with the True One?

ਗੁਰਮੁਖਿ ਅਸਟ ਸਿਧੀ ਸਭਿ ਬੁਧੀ॥
ਗੁਰਮੁਖਿ ਭਵਜਲੁ ਤਰੀਐ ਸਚ ਸੁਧੀ॥
ਗੁਰਮੁਖਿ ਸਰ ਅਪਸਰ ਬਿਧਿ ਜਾਣੈ॥
ਗੁਰਮੁਖਿ ਪਰਵਿਰਤਿ ਨਰਵਿਰਤਿ ਪਛਾਣੈ॥
ਗੁਰਮੁਖਿ ਤਾਰੇ ਪਾਰਿ ਉਤਾਰੇ॥
ਨਾਨਕ ਗੁਰਮੁਖਿ ਸਬਦਿ ਨਿਸਤਾਰੇ॥੩੧॥

Gurmukh ashat sidhi sabh budhi.
Gurmukh bhavjal tareeye sach sudhi.
Gurmukh sar apsar bidhi jaaney.
Gurmukh parvirat narvirat pachhaney.
Gurmukh taarey paar utaarey.
Nanak gurmukh shabad nistaarey. 31.

गुरमुख असट सिधी सभ बुधी।।
गुरमुख भवजल तरीऐ सच सुधी।।
गुरमुख सर अपसर बिधि जाणै।।
गुरमुख परविरत नरविरत पछाणै।।
गुरमुख तारे पार उतारे।।
नानक गुरमुख सबद निसतारे।। 31।।

The *gurmukh* obtains the spiritual powers and all wisdom.
The *gurmukh* crosses the ocean with true knowledge.
The *gurmukh* distinguishes between the true and the false.
The *gurmukh* discrminates between attachment and detachment.
Helped by the Guru, he crosses the ocean and ferries others along.
His secret is that he listens to the all-pervasive Naam.

ਨਾਮੇ ਰਾਤੇ ਹਉਮੈ ਜਾਇ॥

ਨਾਮਿ ਰਤੇ ਸਚਿ ਰਹੇ ਸਮਾਇ॥

ਨਾਮਿ ਰਤੇ ਜੋਗ ਜੁਗਤਿ ਬੀਚਾਰੁ॥

ਨਾਮਿ ਰਤੇ ਪਾਵਹਿ ਮੋਖ ਦੁਆਰੁ॥

ਨਾਮਿ ਰਤੇ ਤ੍ਰਿਭਵਣ ਸੋਝੀ ਹੋਇ॥

ਨਾਨਕ ਨਾਮਿ ਰਤੇ ਸਦਾ ਸੁਖੁ ਹੋਇ॥੩੨॥

Naamey raatey haumei jaaye.

Naam rattey sach rahey samaaye.

Naam rattey jog jugat bichaar.

Naam rattey paavey mokh duaar.

Naam rattey tribhavan sojhi hoye.

Nanak naam rattey sada sukh hoye. 32.

नामे राते हउमै जाए।।
नाम रते सच रहे समाए।।
नाम रते जोग जुगत बीचार।।
नाम रते पावै मोख दुआर।।
नाम रते त्रिभवन सोझी होए।।
नानक नाम रते सदा सुख होए।। 32।।

Immersed in Naam your ego disappears.
Immersed in Naam you become one with the Divine.
Immersed in Naam you succeed in yoga and techniques of meditation.
Immersed in Naam you arrive at the door of liberation.
Immersed in Naam you are aware of the three realms.
Immersed in Naam you are in a state of eternal bliss.

ਨਾਮਿ ਰਤੇ ਸਿਧ ਗੋਸਟਿ ਹੋਇ॥
ਨਾਮਿ ਰਤੇ ਸਦਾ ਤਪ ਹੋਇ॥
ਨਾਮਿ ਰਤੇ ਸਚੁ ਕਰਣੀ ਸਾਰੁ॥
ਨਾਮਿ ਰਤੇ ਗੁਣ ਗਿਆਨ ਬੀਚਾਰੁ॥
ਬਿਨੁ ਨਾਵੈ ਬੋਲੈ ਸਭੁ ਵੇਕਾਰੁ॥
ਨਾਨਕ ਨਾਮਿ ਰਤੇ ਤਿਨ ਕਉ ਜੈਕਾਰੁ॥੩੩॥

Naam rattey sidh gosht hoye.
Naam rattey sada tup hoye.
Naam rattey sach karni saar.
Naam rattey gunn gyaan bichaar.
Bin naavey boley sabh vekaar.
Nanak naam rattey tinn ko jaikaar. 33.

नाम रते सिध गोष्ट होए।।
नाम रते सदा तप होए।।
नाम रते सच करणी सार।।
नाम रते गुण गिआन बीचार।।
बिन नावै बोले सभ वेकार।।
नानक नाम रते तिन को जैकार।। 33।।

Immersed in Naam you can converse with the siddhas.
Immersed in Naam you are always in a state of meditation.
Immersed in Naam you get hold of the essence of truth and truthful living.
Immersed in Naam you arrive at the secret of all knowledge.
Without Naam all you say or do is meaningless.
Salutations to those who are immersed in Naam!

ਪੂਰੇ ਗੁਰ ਤੇ ਨਾਮੁ ਪਾਇਆ ਜਾਇ॥
ਜੋਗ ਜੁਗਤਿ ਸਚਿ ਰਹੈ ਸਮਾਇ॥
ਬਾਰਹ ਮਹਿ ਜੋਗੀ ਭਰਮਾਏ ਸੰਨਿਆਸੀ ਛਿਅ ਚਾਰਿ॥
ਗੁਰ ਕੈ ਸਬਦਿ ਜੋ ਮਰਿ ਜੀਵੈ ਸੋ ਪਾਏ ਮੋਖ ਦੁਆਰੁ॥
ਬਿਨੁ ਸਬਦੈ ਸਭਿ ਦੂਜੈ ਲਾਗੇ ਦੇਖਹੁ ਰਿਦੈ ਬੀਚਾਰਿ॥
ਨਾਨਕ ਵਡੇ ਸੇ ਵਡਭਾਗੀ ਜਿਨੀ ਸਚੁ ਰਖਿਆ ਉਰ ਧਾਰਿ॥੩੪॥

Poorey gur te naam paaya jaaye.
Jog jugat sach rahey samaaye.
Barhe meh jogi bharmaaye sanyasi chhey chaar.
Gur ke shabad jo marr jeevey so paaye mokh duaar.
Bin shabadey sabh dujey laagey dekho ridey bichaar.
Nanak vaddey se vaddbhaagi jinni sach rakhya ur dhaar. 34.

पूरे गुर ते नाम पाया जाए।।
जोग जुगत सच रहै समाए।।
बारह मह जोगी भरमाए सन्यासी छह चार।।
गुर के सबद जो मर जीवै सो पाए मोख दुआर।।
बिन सबदै सभ दूजै लागे देखो रिदै बीचार।।
नानक वडे से वडभागी जिनी सच रखिआ उर धार।। 34।।

You can get to Naam only with the help of the true Guru.
The real yoga is to remain immersed in Naam.
Otherwise the yogis wander in twelve sects and the sannyasis in ten.
Only those who dissolve themselves in Naam get to the door of liberation.
Look within and see that without Naam everyone is engrossed in the world.
Only a few fortunate ones have housed the truth in their hearts.

ਗੁਰਮੁਖਿ ਰਤਨੁ ਲਹੈ ਲਿਵ ਲਾਇ॥
ਗੁਰਮੁਖਿ ਪਰਖੈ ਰਤਨੁ ਸੁਭਾਇ॥
ਗੁਰਮੁਖਿ ਸਾਚੀ ਕਾਰ ਕਮਾਇ॥
ਗੁਰਮੁਖਿ ਸਾਚੇ ਮਨੁ ਪਤੀਆਇ॥
ਗੁਰਮੁਖਿ ਅਲਖੁ ਲਖਾਏ ਤਿਸੁ ਭਾਵੈ॥
ਨਾਨਕ ਗੁਰਮੁਖਿ ਚੋਟ ਨ ਖਾਵੈ॥੩੫॥

Gurmukh rattan lahey liv laaye.
Gurmukh parkhey rattan subhaaye.
Gurmukh saachi kaar kamaaye.
Gurmukh saachey mann pateeaaye.
Gurmukh alakh lakhaye tis bhaavey.
Nanak gurmukh chot na khaavey. 35.

गुरमुख रतन लहै लिव लाए।।
गुरमुख परखे रतन सुभाए।।
गुरमुख साची कार कमाए।।
गुरमुख साचे मन पतिआए।।
गुरमुख अलख लखाए तिस भावै।।
नानक गुरमुख चोट न खावै।। 35।।

Immersed in love the *gurmukh* finds the real pearls.
The *gurmukh* has a connoisseur's eye for the real pearls.
The *gurmukh* lives a life true to his intrinsic nature.
The *gurmukh* is content with pleasing the Divine.
Pleased with the *gurmukh* the Guru gives him the vision of the invisible
The *gurmukh* neither goes astray nor suffers punishment.

ਗੁਰਮੁਖਿ ਨਾਮੁ ਦਾਨੁ ਇਸਨਾਨੁ॥
ਗੁਰਮੁਖਿ ਲਾਗੈ ਸਹਜਿ ਧਿਆਨੁ॥
ਗੁਰਮੁਖਿ ਪਾਵੈ ਦਰਗਹ ਮਾਨੁ॥
ਗੁਰਮੁਖਿ ਭਉ ਭੰਜਨੁ ਪਰਧਾਨੁ॥
ਗੁਰਮੁਖਿ ਕਰਣੀ ਕਾਰ ਕਰਾਏ॥
ਨਾਨਕ ਗੁਰਮੁਖਿ ਮੇਲਿ ਮਿਲਾਏ॥੩੬॥

Gurmukh naam daan isnaan.
Gurmukh laagey sahaj dhyaan.
Gurmukh paavey dargah maan.
Gurmukh bhau bhanjan pardhaan.
Gurmukh karni kaar karaaye.
Nanak gurmukh mel milaaye. 36.

गुरमुख नाम दान इसनान।।
गुरमुख लागै सहज धिआन।।
गुरमुख पावै दरगह मान।।
गुरमुख भउ भँजन परधान।।
गुरमुख करणी कार कराए।।
नानक गुरमुख मेल मिलाए।। 36।।

The *gurmukh* is blessed with Naam, generosity and purity.
The *gurmukh* enters into meditation effortlessly.
The *gurmukh* is honoured in the Divine Court.
The *gurmukh* becomes one with the fearless supreme being.
The *gurmukh* follows the Divine Will and inspires others to do so.
The *gurmukh* dives into divinity and takes others along.

ਗੁਰਮੁਖਿ ਸਾਸਤ੍ਰ ਸਿਮ੍ਰਿਤਿ ਬੇਦ॥
ਗੁਰਮੁਖਿ ਪਾਵੈ ਘਟਿ ਘਟਿ ਭੇਦ॥
ਗੁਰਮੁਖਿ ਵੈਰ ਵਿਰੋਧ ਗਵਾਵੈ॥
ਗੁਰਮੁਖਿ ਸਗਲੀ ਗਣਤ ਮਿਟਾਵੈ॥
ਗੁਰਮੁਖਿ ਰਾਮ ਨਾਮ ਰੰਗਿ ਰਾਤਾ॥
ਨਾਨਕ ਗੁਰਮੁਖਿ ਖਸਮੁ ਪਛਾਤਾ॥੩੭॥

Gurmukh shastar simrat ved.
Gurmukh paavey ghat ghat bhed.
Gurmukh vair virodh gavaavey.
Gurmukh sagli ganat mitaavey.
Gurmukh Ram naam rang raata.
Nanak gurmukh khasam pachhaata. 37.

गुरमुख सासत्र सिमरत बेद।।
गुरमुख पावै घट घट भेद।।
गुरमुख वैर विरोध गवावै।।
गुरमुख सगली गणत मिटावै।।
गुरमुख राम नाम रँग राता।।
नानक गुरमुख खसम पछाता।। 37।।

The *gurmukh* knows all Vedas and scriptures.
The *gurmukh* detects the underlying divinity in all creatures.
The *gurmukh* has no enemies or enmity
The *gurmukh* closes all accounts of good and bad, give and take.
The *gurmukh* is imbued in the hues of Naam.
The *gurmukh* has recognised the true Lord.

ਬਿਨੁ ਗੁਰ ਭਰਮੈ ਆਵੈ ਜਾਇ॥
ਬਿਨੁ ਗੁਰ ਘਾਲ ਨ ਪਵਈ ਥਾਇ॥
ਬਿਨੁ ਗੁਰ ਮਨੂਆ ਅਤਿ ਡੋਲਾਇ॥
ਬਿਨੁ ਗੁਰ ਤ੍ਰਿਪਤਿ ਨਹੀ ਬਿਖੁ ਖਾਇ॥
ਬਿਨੁ ਗੁਰ ਬਿਸੀਅਰੁ ਡਸੈ ਮਰਿ ਵਾਟ॥
ਨਾਨਕ ਬਿਨੁ ਗੁਰ ਘਾਟੇ ਘਾਟ॥੩੮॥

Bin gur bharmey aavey jaaye.
Bin gur ghaal na pavyee thaaye.
Bin gur manua ati dolaaye.
Bin gur tripat nahi bikh khaaye.
Bin gur bisiar dassey marr vaat.
Nanak bin gur ghaatey ghaat. 38.

बिन गुर भरमे आवै जाए।।
बिन गुर घाल न पवई थाए।।
बिन गुर मनूआ अति डोलाए।।
बिन गुर तृपत नहीं बिख खाए।।
बिन गुर बिसीअर डसै मर वाट।।
नानक बिन गुर घाटै घाट।। 38।।

Without the Guru, you come and go round in circles.
Without the Guru all your efforts go waste.
Without the Guru your mind wavers incessantly.
Without the Guru you are never satisfied; indeed you are poisoned.
Without the Guru you are bitten by the serpent, maya, and you perish.
Without the Guru everything comes to naught and all is lost.

ਜਿਸੁ ਗੁਰੁ ਮਿਲੈ ਤਿਸੁ ਪਾਰਿ ਉਤਾਰੈ॥
ਅਵਗਣ ਮੇਟੈ ਗੁਣਿ ਨਿਸਤਾਰੈ॥
ਮੁਕਤਿ ਮਹਾ ਸੁਖ ਗੁਰ ਸਬਦੁ ਬੀਚਾਰਿ॥
ਗੁਰਮੁਖਿ ਕਦੇ ਨ ਆਵੈ ਹਾਰਿ॥
ਤਨੁ ਹਟੜੀ ਇਹੁ ਮਨੁ ਵਣਜਾਰਾ॥
ਨਾਨਕ ਸਹਜੇ ਸਚੁ ਵਾਪਾਰਾ॥੩੯॥

Jis guru miley tis paar utaarey.
Avgann metey gunn nistaarey.
Mukat maha sukh gur shabad bichaar.
Gurmukh kadey na aavey haar.
Tann hatrhi eh mann vanjaara.
Nanak sahajey sach vapaara. 39.

जिस गुर मिलै तिस पार उतारे।।
अवगण मेटे गुण निसतारे।।
मुकत महा सुख गुर सबद बीचार।।
गुरमुख कदे न आवै हार।।
तन हटड़ी इह मन वनजारा।।
नानक सहजे सच वापारा।। 39।।

One who meets the Guru is ferried across.
His account of sins is closed and he is saved by his virtues.
Attuned to the Guru's word he attains eternal peace.
Such a *gurmukh* is never defeated.
In the store of the body his mind is the trader
Who trades in the existential truth of Naam.

ਗੁਰਮੁਖਿ ਬਾਂਧਿਓ ਸੇਤੁ ਬਿਧਾਤੈ॥
ਲੰਕਾ ਲੂਟੀ ਦੈਤ ਸੰਤਾਪੈ॥
ਰਾਮਚੰਦਿ ਮਾਰਿਓ ਅਹਿ ਰਾਵਣੁ॥
ਭੇਦੁ ਬਭੀਖਣ ਗੁਰਮੁਖਿ ਪਰਚਾਇਣੁ॥
ਗੁਰਮੁਖਿ ਸਾਇਰਿ ਪਾਹਣ ਤਾਰੇ॥
ਗੁਰਮੁਖਿ ਕੋਟਿ ਤੇਤੀਸ ਉਧਾਰੇ॥੪੦॥

Gurmukh baandheyo seit bidhaatey.
Lanka lootee dait santaapey.
Ramchand maaryo ahe Ravan.
Bhed Babheekhan gurmukh parchayan.
Gurmukh sayar paahan taarey.
Gurmukh kot taitees udhaarey. 40.

गुरमुख बांधियो सेत बिधातै।।
लँका लूटी दैत सँतापै।।
रामचंद तारियो अह रावण।।
भेख बभीखण गुरमुख परचायण।।
गुरमुख सायर पाहण तारे।।
गुरमुख कोट तेतीस उधारे।। 40।।

The *gurmukh* is the bridge built by the Creator.
The *gurmukh* is like Rama who conquered Ravana, the ego.
He defeated the demons of lust who were robbing the body (Lanka).
The Gurmukh understood the secret revealed by Babheekhana.
The Gurmukh like Rama blessed the stones also and liberated them.
The Gurmukh saved millions and led them from bondage to freedom.

ਗੁਰਮੁਖਿ ਚੂਕੈ ਆਵਣ ਜਾਣੁ॥
ਗੁਰਮੁਖਿ ਦਰਗਹ ਪਾਵੈ ਮਾਣੁ॥
ਗੁਰਮੁਖਿ ਖੋਟੇ ਖਰੇ ਪਛਾਣੁ॥
ਗੁਰਮੁਖਿ ਲਾਗੈ ਸਹਜਿ ਧਿਆਨੁ॥
ਗੁਰਮੁਖਿ ਦਰਗਹ ਸਿਫਤਿ ਸਮਾਇ॥
ਨਾਨਕ ਗੁਰਮੁਖਿ ਬੰਧ ਨ ਪਾਇ॥ ੪੧

Gurmukh chookey aavan jaan.
Gurmukh dargah paavey maan.
Gurmukh khotey kharey pachhaan.
Gurmukh laagey sahaj dhyaan.
Gurmukh dargah sifat samaaye.
Nanak guurmukh bandh na paaye. 41.

गुरमुख चूकै आवण जाण।।
गुरमुख दरगह पावै माण।।
गुरमुख खोटे खरे पछाण।।
गुरमुख लागै सहज धिआन।।
गुरमुख दरगह सिफत समाए।।
नानक गुरमुख बँध न पाए।। 41।।

The *gurmukh* is out of the cycle of birth and death.
The *gurmukh* is honoured in the Divine Court.
The *gurmukh* distinguishes between the true and the false.
The *gurmukh* enters into meditation effortlessly.
The *gurmukh* remains absorbed in praise of the Divine.
The *gurmukh* is beyond the grip of bondage of any kind.

ਗੁਰਮੁਖਿ ਨਾਮੁ ਨਿਰੰਜਨ ਪਾਏ॥
ਗੁਰਮੁਖਿ ਹਉਮੈ ਸਬਦਿ ਜਲਾਏ॥
ਗੁਰਮੁਖਿ ਸਾਚੇ ਕੇ ਗੁਣ ਗਾਏ॥
ਗੁਰਮੁਖਿ ਸਾਚੈ ਰਹੈ ਸਮਾਏ॥
ਗੁਰਮੁਖਿ ਸਾਚਿ ਨਾਮਿ ਪਤਿ ਊਤਮ ਹੋਇ॥
ਨਾਨਕ ਗੁਰਮੁਖਿ ਸਗਲ ਭਵਣ ਕੀ ਸੋਝੀ ਹੋਇ॥੪੨॥

Gurmukh naam niranjan paaye.
Gurmukh haumei shabad jalaaye.
Gurmukh saachey ke gunn gaaye.
Gurmukh saachey rahey samaaye.
Gurmukh saach naam patt oottam hoye.
Nanak gurmukh sagal bhavan ki sojhi hoye. 42.

गुरमुख नाम निरँजन पाए।।
गुरमुख हउमै सबद जलाए।।
गुरमुख साचे के गुण गाए।।
गुरमुख साचे रहै समाए।।
गुरमुख साच नाम पत ऊतम होए।।
नानक गुरमुख सगल भवन की सोझी होए।। 42।।

The *gurmukh* attains the all-pervading Naam.
The *gurmukh* burns his ego with the Guru's word.
The *gurmukh* sings of the divine qualities
Thus the *gurmukh* imbibes those qualities in himself.
The *gurmukh* is praised though he remains absorbed in Naam.
The *gurmukh* is aware of all the realms of existence.

ਕਵਣ ਮੂਲ ਕਵਣ ਮਤਿ ਵੇਲਾ।।

ਤੇਰਾ ਕਵਣੁ ਗੁਰੁ ਜਿਸ ਕਾ ਤੂ ਚੇਲਾ।।

ਕਵਣ ਕਥਾ ਲੇ ਰਹਹੁ ਨਿਰਾਲੇ।।

ਬੋਲੈ ਨਾਨਕ ਸੁਣਹੁ ਤੁਮ ਬਾਲੇ।।

ਏਸੁ ਕਥਾ ਕਾ ਦੇਇ ਬੀਚਾਰੁ।।

ਭਵਜਲੁ ਸਬਦਿ ਲੰਘਾਵਣਹਾਰੁ।।੪੩।।

Kavan mool kavan matt vela.

Tera kavan guru jis ka tu chela.

Kavan katha lei raho niraaley.

Boley Nanak sunnho tum baaley.

Eis katha ka dei bichaar.

Bhavjal shabad langhaavanhaar. 43.

कवण मूल कवण मत वेला।।
तेरा कवण गुरू जिस का तू चेला।।
कवण कथा ले रहो निराले।।
बोलै नानक सुणो तुम बाले।।
एस कथा का तुम दे बीचार।।
भवजल सबद लँघावणहार।। 43।।

Question: "Where is the source of your knowledge?
Which religion do you follow?
Who is your Guru? Whose disciple are you?
What is your philosophy that makes you detached?
Though young in years, give us your opinion
How can Naam help us cross the bridge from bondage to freedom?"

ਪਵਨ ਅਰੰਭ ਸਤਿਗੁਰ ਮਤਿ ਵੇਲਾ॥
ਸਬਦੁ ਗੁਰੂ ਸੁਰਤਿ ਧੁਨਿ ਚੇਲਾ॥
ਅਕਥ ਕਥਾ ਲੇ ਰਹਉ ਨਿਰਾਲਾ॥
ਨਾਨਕ ਜੁਗਿ ਜੁਗਿ ਗੁਰ ਗੋਪਾਲਾ॥
ਏਕੁ ਸਬਦੁ ਜਿਤੁ ਕਥਾ ਵੀਚਾਰੀ॥
ਗੁਰਮੁਖਿ ਹਉਮੈ ਅਗਨਿ ਨਿਵਾਰੀ॥੪੪॥

Pavan arambh satgur matt vela.
Shabad guru surat dhun chela.
Akath katha lei raho niraala.
Nanak jug jug gur gopaala.
Ek shabad jit katha vichaaree.
Gurmukh haumei agan nivaaree. 44.

पवन अरँभ सतगुर मत वेला।।
सबद गुरू सुरत धुन चेला।।
अकथ कथा ले रहो निराला।।
नानक जुग जुग गुर गोपाला।।
एक सबद जित कथा वीचारी।।
गुरमुख हउमै अगन निवारी।। 44।।

Answer: "The life-breath is the beginning of existence,
The word of the Guru is the religion.
Naam is the Guru and my consciousness is the disciple.
I remain detached from the world by attaching my consciousness to the Divine.
This thread of consciousness runs through the ages.
It is only through Naam that we can come to this truth.
The *gurmukh* is enlightened when he burns his ego in the fire."

ਮੈਣ ਕੇ ਦੰਤ ਕਿਉ ਖਾਈਐ ਸਾਰੁ॥
ਜਿਤੁ ਗਰਬੁ ਜਾਇ ਸੁ ਕਵਣੁ ਆਹਾਰੁ॥
ਹਿਵੈ ਕਾ ਘਰੁ ਮੰਦਰੁ ਅਗਨਿ ਪਿਰਾਹਨੁ॥
ਕਵਨ ਗੁਫਾ ਜਿਤੁ ਰਹੈ ਅਵਾਹਨੁ॥
ਇਤ ਉਤ ਕਿਸ ਕਉ ਜਾਣਿ ਸਮਾਵੈ॥
ਕਵਨ ਧਿਆਨੁ ਮਨੁ ਮਨਹਿ ਸਮਾਵੈ॥੪੫॥

Main ke dant kyun khaayeeye saar.
Jit garab jaaye so kavan aahaar.
Hivey ka ghar mandar agan piraahan.
Kavan gufa jit rahey avaahan.
It ut kis ko jaan samaavey.
Kavan dhyaan mann maneh samaavey. 45.

मैण के दँत क्यों खाईए सार।।
जित गरब जाए सु कवण आहार।।
हिवै का घर मँदर अगन पिराहन।।
कवन गुफा जित रहै अवाहन।।
इत उत किस को जाण समावै।।
कवन धिआन मन मनहि समावै।। 45।।

Question:"How can we chew iron (kill the ego) with teeth of wax (inner weakness)?
What is the food that can strengthen the will to kill the ego?
How can we live in the home of snow wearing clothes of fire?
Where is the cave within which we may remain unshaken?
How do we recognise the one that pervades here, there, everywhere?
What is the method by which our mind can remain absorbed in itself?"

ਹਉ ਹਉ ਮੈ ਮੈ ਵਿਚਹੁ ਖੋਵੈ॥
ਦੂਜਾ ਮੇਟੈ ਏਕੋ ਹੋਵੈ॥
ਜਗੁ ਕਰੜਾ ਮਨਮੁਖੁ ਗਾਵਾਰੁ॥
ਸਬਦੁ ਕਮਾਈਐ ਖਾਈਐ ਸਾਰੁ॥
ਅੰਤਰਿ ਬਾਹਰਿ ਏਕੋ ਜਾਣੈ॥
ਨਾਨਕ ਅਗਨਿ ਮਰੈ ਸਤਿਗੁਰ ਕੈ ਭਾਣੈ॥੪੬॥

Hau hau mai mai vichoh khovey.
Duja metey eko hovey.
Jag kararha manmukh gavaar.
Shabad kamaayeeye khayeeye saar.
Antar bahar eko jaaney.
Nanak agan marrey satgur ke bhaaney. 46.

हउ हउ मै मै विचों खोवै।।
दूजा मेटे एको होवै।।
जग करड़ा मनमुख गावार।।
सबद कमाईए खाईए सार।।
अँतर बाहर एको जाणै।।
नानक अगन मरै सतगुर कै भाणे।। 46।।

Answer: "Remove egoism from the very root.
Demolish all dualities and become one by identifying with the One
The world of maya seems daunting to the weak-willed *manmukh.*
Practise identification with Naam to be able to chew iron.
Remember that there is only the True One that permeates in and out.
Ultimately it is the Guru's blessings that will extinguish the fire of ego."

ਸਚ ਭੈ ਰਾਤਾ ਗਰੁਬ ਨਿਵਾਰੈ॥
ਏਕੋ ਜਾਤਾ ਸਬਦੁ ਵੀਚਾਰੈ॥
ਸਬਦੁ ਵਸੈ ਸਚੁ ਅੰਤਰਿ ਹੀਆ॥
ਤਨੁ ਮਨੁ ਸੀਤਲੁ ਰੰਗਿ ਰੰਗੀਆ॥
ਕਾਮੁ ਕ੍ਰੋਧੁ ਬਿਖੁ ਅਗਨਿ ਨਿਵਾਰੇ॥
ਨਾਨਕ ਨਦਰੀ ਨਦਰਿ ਪਿਆਰੇ॥੪੭॥

Sach bhay raata garab nivaarey.
Eko jaata shabad vichaarey.
Shabad vassey sach antar heeya.
Tann mann seetal rang rangeeya.
Kaam krodh bikh agan nivaarey.
Nanak nadree nadar pyaarey. 47.

सच भै राता गरब निवारै।।
एको जाता सबद वीचारै।।
सबद वसै सच अँतर हीआ।।
तन मन सीतल रँग रँगीआ।।
काम क्रोध बिख अगन निवारे।।
नानक नदरी नदर पिआरे।। 47।।

"Drown yourself in the True One and the ego will be dissolved.
Let the Guru's word penetrate your heart.
When Naam begins to reside in your heart,
Your body and mind will also get coloured by it.
And the fire of lust, anger, venom will cool down.
With His loving grace you too will overflow with love."

ਕਵਨ ਮੁਖਿ ਚੰਦੁ ਹਿਵੈ ਘਰੁ ਛਾਇਆ॥
ਕਵਨ ਮੁਖਿ ਸੂਰਜ ਤਪੈ ਤਪਾਇਆ॥
ਕਵਨ ਮੁਖਿ ਕਾਲੁ ਜੋਹਤ ਨਿਤ ਰਹੈ॥
ਕਵਨ ਬੁਧਿ ਗੁਰਮੁਖਿ ਪਤਿ ਰਹੈ॥
ਕਵਨ ਜੋਧੁ ਜੋ ਕਾਲੁ ਸੰਘਾਰੈ॥
ਬੋਲੈ ਬਾਣੀ ਨਾਨਕ ਬੀਚਾਰੈ॥੪੮॥

Kavan mukh chand hivey ghar chhaaya.
Kavan mukh suraj tapey tapaaya.
Kavan mukh kaal johat nitt rahey.
Kavan budhi gurmukh patt rahey.
Kavan jodha jo kaal sanghaarey.
Boley baani Nanak bichaarey. 48.

कवन मुख चँद हिवै घर छाया।।
कवन मुख सूरज तपै तपाया।।
कवन मुख काल जोहत नित रहै।।
कवन बुध गुरमुख पत रहै।।
कवन जोध जो काल सँघारै।।
बोलै बाणी नानक बीचारै।। 48।।

Question: "How does the moon (mind) remain frozen and dark?
What makes the sun (consciousness) bright and brilliant?
What is the way to turn the watchful gaze of death away?
What is the method to acquire the attitude of *gurmukh*?
Who is the warrior that can conquer death and mortality?
Tell us what is your opinion on these matters."

ਸਬਦੁ ਭਾਖਤ ਸਸਿ ਜੋਤਿ ਅਪਾਰਾ॥
ਸਸਿ ਘਰਿ ਸੂਰੁ ਵਸੈ ਮਿਟੈ ਅੰਧਿਆਰਾ॥
ਸੁਖੁ ਦੁਖੁ ਸਮ ਕਰਿ ਨਾਮੁ ਅਧਾਰਾ॥
ਆਪੇ ਪਾਰਿ ਉਤਾਰਣਹਾਰਾ॥
ਗੁਰ ਪਰਚੈ ਮਨੁ ਸਾਚਿ ਸਮਾਇ॥
ਪ੍ਰਣਵਤਿ ਨਾਨਕ ਕਾਲੁ ਨ ਖਾਇ॥੪੯॥

Shabad bhaakhat sasi jot apaara.
Sasi ghar soor vassey mitey andhyaara.
Sukh dukh sum kar naam adhaara.
Aapey paar utaaranhaara.
Gur parchey mann saach samaaye.
Pranvatt Nanak kaal na khaaye. 49.

सबद भाखत ससि जोत अपारा।।
ससि घर सूर वसै मिटै अँधिआरा।।
सुख दुख सम कर नाम अधारा।।
आपे पार उतारणहारा।।
गुर परचै मन साच समाए।।
प्रणवत नानक काल न खाए।। 49।।

"Naam is the sunlight that dispels darkness from the heart.
When the moon absorbs the sunlight it gets illuminated.
This light shows you that joys and sorrows are two sides of the same coin.
This understanding comes from the Creator who alone can bestow it.
Following the path led by the Guru you remain immersed in divinity.
Then there is no death or the fear of coming and going again.

ਨਾਮ ਤਤੁ ਸਭ ਹੀ ਸਿਰਿ ਜਾਪੈ॥
ਬਿਨੁ ਨਾਵੈ ਕਾਲੁ ਸੰਤਾਪੈ॥
ਤਤੋ ਤਤੁ ਮਿਲੈ ਮਨੁ ਮਾਨੈ॥
ਦੂਜਾ ਜਾਇ ਇਕਤੁ ਘਰਿ ਆਨੈ॥
ਬੋਲੈ ਪਵਨਾ ਗਗਨੁ ਗਰਜੈ॥
ਨਾਨਕ ਨਿਹਚਲੁ ਮਿਲਣੁ ਸਹਜੈ॥੫੦॥

Naam tatt sabh hi sir jaapey.
Bin naavey kaal santaapey.
Tatto tatt miley mann maaney.
Duja jaaye ikkat ghar aaney.
Boley pavna gagan garjey.
Nanak nehchal milan sahajey. 50.

नाम तत सभ ही सिर जापै।।

बिन नावै काल सँतापै।।

ततो तत मिलै मन मानै।।

दूजा जाए इकत घर आनै।।

बोलै पवना गगन गरजै।।

नानक निहचल मिलण सहजै।। 50।।

Naam is the pinnacle where the soul and the source are one.

Without Naam there is always the fear and anxiety of death.

When the part dissolves in the whole you have come home.

Then all dualities disappear and only one remains.

Then life flows through you like air in a flute making music.

This is the state of being when you are grounded in yourself naturally.

ਅੰਤਰਿ ਸੁੰਨੰ ਬਾਹਰਿ ਸੁੰਨੰ ਤ੍ਰਿਭਵਣ ਸੁੰਨ ਮਸੁੰਨੰ।।
ਚਉਥੇ ਸੁੰਨੈ ਜੋ ਨਰੁ ਜਾਣੈ ਤਾ ਕਉ ਪਾਪੁ ਨ ਪੁੰਨੰ।।
ਘਟਿ ਘਟਿ ਸੁੰਨ ਕਾ ਜਾਣੈ ਭੇਉ।।
ਆਦਿ ਪੁਰਖੁ ਨਿਰੰਜਨ ਦੇਉ।।
ਜੋ ਜਨੁ ਨਾਮ ਨਿਰੰਜਨ ਰਾਤਾ।।
ਨਾਨਕ ਸੋਈ ਪੁਰਖੁ ਬਿਧਾਤਾ।।੫੧।।

Antar sunnam bahar sunnam tribhavan sunn masunnam.
Chauthey sunney jo nar jaaney ta ko paap na punnam.
Ghat ghat sunn ka jaaney bheo.
Aad purakh niranjan deo.
Jo jan naam niranjan raata.
Nanak soyee purakh bidhaata. 51.

अँतर सुँनँ बाहर सुँनँ त्रिभवन सुँन मसुँनँ।।
चौथे सुँनै जो नर जाणै ता का पाप न पुँनँ।।
घट घट सुँन का जाणै भेउ।।
आद पुरख निरँजन देउ।।
जो जन नाम निरँजन राता।।
नानक सोई पुरख बिधाता।। 51।।

The unstruck sound of silence pervades in and out and in the three realms
But, he who knows the fourth state, rises above virtues and vices.
When you hear the all-pervading sound of silence in your heart
You have become one with the formless deity.
He who is thus absorbed in the formless divinity
He alone is the Supreme Creator."

ਸੁੰਨੋ ਸੁੰਨ ਕਹੈ ਸਭੁ ਕੋਈ॥
ਅਨਹਤ ਸੁੰਨੁ ਕਹਾ ਤੇ ਹੋਈ॥
ਅਨਹਤ ਸੁਨਿ ਰਤੇ ਸੇ ਕੈਸੇ॥
ਜਿਸ ਤੇ ਉਪਜੇ ਤਿਸ ਹੀ ਜੈਸੇ॥
ਓਇ ਜਨਮਿ ਨ ਮਰਹਿ ਨ ਆਵਹਿ ਜਾਹਿ॥
ਨਾਨਕ ਗੁਰਮੁਖਿ ਮਨੁ ਸਮਝਾਹਿ ॥੫੨॥

Sunno sunn kahey sabh koyee.
Anhat sunn kaha te hoyee.
Anhat sunn rattey se kaisey.
Jis te upjey tis hi jaisey.
Oye janam na mareh na aaveh jaahey.
Nanak gurmukh mann samjhaaye. 52.

सुँनो सुँन कहै सभ कोई।।
अनहत सुँन कहा ते होई।।
अनहत सुन रते से कैसे।।
जिस ते उपजै तिस ही जैसे।।
ओए जनम न मरे न आवे जाए।।
नानक गुरमुख मन समझाए।। 52।।

Question: "Everyone talks about this state of *shunya*
But how does one arrive at this state of being?
What do they look like who have achieved this state?"

Answer: "They are like the Creator who has created them.
They are beyond the cycle of birth and death, they don't come and go.
They have attained this state of being with the Guru's guidance.

ਨਉ ਸਰ ਸੁਭਰ ਦਸਵੈ ਪੂਰੇ॥
ਤਹ ਅਨਹਤ ਸੁੰਨ ਵਜਾਵਹਿ ਤੂਰੇ॥
ਸਾਚੈ ਰਾਚੇ ਦੇਖਿ ਹਜੂਰੇ॥
ਘਟਿ ਘਟਿ ਸਾਚੁ ਰਹਿਆ ਭਰਪੂਰੇ॥
ਗੁਪਤੀ ਬਾਣੀ ਪਰਗਟੁ ਹੋਇ॥
ਨਾਨਕ ਪਰਖਿ ਲਏ ਸਚੁ ਸੋਇ॥੫੩॥

Nau sar subhar dasvey poorey.
Teh anhat sunn vajaveh toorey.
Saachey raachey dekh hajoorey.
Ghat ghat saach rahya bharpoorey.
Gupti baani pargat hoye.
Nanak parakh laye sach soye. 53.

नौ सर सुभर दसवै पूरे।।
तह अनहत सुँन वजावे तूरे।।
साचै राचे देख हजूरे।।
घट घट साच रहिआ भरपूरे।।
गुपती बाणी परगट होए।।
नानक परख लए सच सोए।। 53।।

Nine gates lead the mind outwards; only the tenth takes you in.
That is where you can hear the unstruck sound of Naam.
That is where you can see the Creator face to face.
You can see the One that lives in everyone and everything.
Then that which is hidden is revealed.
You can try and test it and verify it for yourself.

ਸਹਜ ਭਾਇ ਮਿਲੀਐ ਸੁਖੁ ਹੋਵੈ॥
ਗੁਰਮੁਖਿ ਜਾਗੈ ਨੀਦ ਨ ਸੋਵੈ॥
ਸੁੰਨ ਸਬਦੁ ਅਪਰੰਪਰਿ ਧਾਰੈ॥
ਕਹਤੇ ਮੁਕਤੁ ਸਬਦਿ ਨਿਸਤਾਰੈ॥
ਗੁਰ ਕੀ ਦੀਖਿਆ ਸੇ ਸਚਿ ਰਾਤੇ॥
ਨਾਨਕ ਆਪੁ ਗਵਾਇ ਮਿਲਣ ਨਹੀ ਭ੍ਰਾਤੇ॥੫੪॥

Sahaj bhaaye miliye sukh hovey.
Gurmukh jaagey neend na sovey.
Sunn shabad aparampar dhaarey.
Kahtey mukat shabad nistaarey.
Gur ki deekhiya se sach raatey.
Nanak aap gavaaye milan nahi bhraatey. 54.

सहज भाए मिलिए सुख होवै।।
गुरमुख जागै नींद न सोवै।।
सुँन सबद अपरँपर धारै।।
कहते मुकत सबद निसतारै।।
गुर की दीखिआ से सच राते।।
नानक आप गवाए मिलण नहीं भ्राते।। 54।।

When you unite naturally then only you are at peace.
Then you remain conscious all the time, even in sleep.
Then you hear the continuous sound of Naam resounding within.
Then you are liberated and you take many along.
Then the Guru's word is the ocean in which you dissolve yourself.
Without such dissolution no union is possible."

ਕੁਬੁਧਿ ਚਵਾਵੈ ਸੋ ਕਿਤੁ ਠਾਇ॥
ਕਿਉ ਤਤੁ ਨ ਬੂਝੈ ਚੋਟਾ ਖਾਇ॥
ਜਮ ਦਰਿ ਬਾਧੇ ਕੋਇ ਨ ਰਾਖੈ॥
ਬਿਨੁ ਸਬਦੈ ਨਾਹੀ ਪਤਿ ਸਾਖੈ॥
ਕਿਉ ਕਰਿ ਬੂਝੈ ਪਾਵੈ ਪਾਰੁ॥
ਨਾਨਕ ਮਨਮੁਖਿ ਨ ਬੁਝੈ ਗਵਾਰੁ॥੫੫॥

Kubudh chavaavey so kitt thaaye.
Kyun tatt na bhoojhey chota khaaye.
Jamm dar baadhey koye na raakhey.
Bin shabadey naahi patt saakhey.
Kyun kar boojhey paavey paar.
Nanak manmukh na bujhey gavaar. 55.

कुबुध चवावै सो कित ठाए।।
क्यों तत न बूझै चोटां खाए।।
जम दर बाधे कोए न राखै।।
बिन सबदै नाही पत साखै।।
क्यों कर बुझै पावै पार।।
नानक मनमुख न बुझै गवार।। 55।।

Question: "What is the fate of the ignorant person who talks nonsense?"

Answer: "Without realising the basic truth he suffers pain.
He is imprisoned by death and no one comes to his rescue.
Without Naam he has no respect or honour."

Question: "How can such a person find the path to liberation?"
Answer: "Such a self-willed foolish person refuses to understand."

ਕੁਬੁਧਿ ਮਿਟੈ ਗੁਰ ਸਬਦੁ ਬੀਚਾਰਿ॥
ਸਤਿਗੁਰੁ ਭੇਟੈ ਮੋਖ ਦੁਆਰ॥
ਤਤੁ ਨ ਚੀਨੈ ਮਨਮੁਖੁ ਜਲਿ ਜਾਇ॥
ਦੁਰਮਤਿ ਵਿਛੁੜਿ ਚੋਟਾ ਖਾਇ॥
ਮਾਨੈ ਹੁਕਮੁ ਸਭੇ ਗੁਣ ਗਿਆਨ॥
ਨਾਨਕ ਦਰਗਹ ਪਾਵੈ ਮਾਨੁ॥੫੬॥

Kubudh mittey gur shabad bichaar.
Satgur bhetey mokh duaar.
Tatt na cheeney manmukh jal jaaye.
Durmat vichhurh chota khaaye.
Maaney hukam sabhey gunn gyaan.
Nanak dargah paavey maan. 56.

कुबुध मिटे गुर सबद बीचार।।
सतगुर भेटे मोख दुआर।।
तत न चीनै मनमुख जल जाए।।
दुरमत विछुड़ चोटा खाए।।
मानै हुकम सभे गुण गिआन।।
नानक दरगह पावै मान।। 56।।

Answer continued: "Ignorance is dispelled by the Guru's word.
The door to liberation opens when you meet the Guru.
The *manmukh* does not see the reality therefore he suffers pain.
It is his wanton mind that separates him from the True One.
If only he would follow the *hukam* he would gain all wisdom.
And he would gain respect and honour in the Divine Court.

ਸਾਚੁ ਵਖਰੁ ਧਨੁ ਪਲੈ ਹੋਇ॥
ਆਪਿ ਤਰੈ ਤਾਰੇ ਭੀ ਸੋਇ॥
ਸਹਜਿ ਰਤਾ ਬੂਝੈ ਪਤਿ ਹੋਇ॥
ਤਾ ਕੀ ਕੀਮਤਿ ਕਰੈ ਨ ਕੋਇ॥
ਜਹ ਦੇਖਾ ਤਹ ਰਹਿਆ ਸਮਾਇ॥
ਨਾਨਕ ਪਾਰਿ ਪਰੈ ਸਚ ਭਾਇ॥੫੭॥

Saach vakhar dhan palley hoye.
Aap tarey taarey bhi soye.
Sahaj ratta boojhey patt hoye.
Ta ki kimat karey na koye.
Jeh dekha teh rahya samaaye.
Nanak paar parey sach bhaaye. 57.

साच वखर धन पलै होए।।
आप तरै तारे भी सोए।।
सहज रता बूझै पत होए।।
ता की कीमत करै न कोए।।
जह देखां तह रहिआ समाए।।
नानक पार परै सच भाए।। 57।।

If you have the true wealth of Naam
You will cross the ocean effortlessly and ferry others along.
If you accept everything as it is you will be honoured.
Then you become worthy of the ultimate.
Then wherever you look you see the Divine.
Then you remain immersed in the ocean of love."

ਸੁ ਸਬਦ ਕਾ ਕਹਾ ਵਾਸੁ ਕਥੀਅਲੇ ਜਿਤੁ ਤਰੀਐ ਭਵਜਲੁ ਸੰਸਾਰੋ॥

ਤ੍ਰੈ ਸਤ ਅੰਗੁਲ ਵਾਈ ਕਹੀਐ ਤਿਸੁ ਕਹੁ ਕਵਨ ਅਧਾਰੋ॥

ਬੋਲੈ ਖੇਲੈ ਅਸਥਿਰੁ ਹੋਵੈ ਕਿਉ ਕਰਿ ਅਲਖ ਲਖਾਏ॥

ਸੁਣਿ ਸੁਆਮੀ ਸਚੁ ਨਾਨਕੁ ਪ੍ਰਣਵੈ ਅਪਣੇ ਮਨ ਸਮਝਾਏ॥

ਗੁਰਮੁਖਿ ਸਬਦੇ ਸਚਿ ਲਿਵ ਲਾਗੈ ਕਰਿ ਨਦਰੀ ਮੇਲਿ ਮਿਲਾਏ॥

ਆਪੇ ਦਾਨਾ ਆਪੇ ਬੀਨਾ ਪੂਰੈ ਭਾਗਿ ਸਮਾਏ॥੫੮॥

So shabad ka kaha vaas kathialey jit tareeye bhavjal sansaaro.

Trai sat angul vaayee kaheeye tis kaho kavan adhaaro.

Boley kheley asthir hovey kyun kar alakh lakhaaye.

Sunn soami sach Nanak pranvey apney mann samjhaaye.

Gurmukh shabadey sach liv laagey kar nadri mel milaaye.

Aapey dana aapey bina poorey bhaag samaaye. 58.

सु सबद का कहा वास कथीअले जित तरीए भवजल सँसारो।।
त्रै सत अँगुल वाई कहीए तिस कहो कवन अधारो।।
बोलै खेलै असथिर होवै क्यों कर अलख लखाए।।
सुन सुआमी सच नानक प्रणवै अपणे मन समझाए।।
गुरमुख सबदे सच लिव लागै कर नदरी मेल मिलाए।।
आपे दाना आपे बीना पूरै भाग समाए।। 58।।

Question: "Tell us about the abode of Naam which can ferry us across.
What is the support of the breath that when exhaled extends only ten fingers in length?
How can this vibrating and wavering breath which moves all else show us the invisible?"

Answer: "O, Swami! All you need to do is to explain it to your mind.
When the *gurmukh* dissolves himself in Naam he is united by His Grace.
For the Divine is the knower and the observer: Only the fortunate realise it.

ਸੁ ਸਬਦ ਕਉ ਨਿਰੰਤਰਿ ਵਾਸੁ ਅਲਖੰ ਜਹ ਦੇਖਾ ਤਹ ਸੋਈ॥
ਪਵਨ ਕਾ ਵਾਸਾ ਸੁੰਨ ਨਿਵਾਸਾ ਅਕਲ ਕਲਾ ਧਰ ਸੋਈ॥
ਨਦਰਿ ਕਰੇ ਸਬਦੁ ਘਟ ਮਹਿ ਵਸੈ ਵਿਚਹੁ ਭਰਮੁ ਗਵਾਏ॥
ਤਨੁ ਮਨੁ ਨਿਰਮਲੁ ਨਿਰਮਲ ਬਾਣੀ ਨਾਮੋ ਮੰਨਿ ਵਸਾਏ॥
ਸਬਦਿ ਗੁਰੁ ਭਵਸਾਗਰੁ ਤਰੀਐ ਇਤ ਉਤ ਏਕੋ ਜਾਣੈ॥
ਚਿਹਨੁ ਵਰਨੁ ਨਹੀ ਛਾਇਆ ਮਾਇਆ ਨਾਨਕ ਸਬਦੁ ਪਛਾਣੈ॥੫੯॥

So shabad ko nirantar vaas alakham jeh dekha teh soyee.
Pavan ka vaasa sunn nivaasa akal kala dhar soyee.
Nadar karey shabad ghat meh vasey vicho bharam gavaaye.
Tann mann nirmal nirmal baani naamo mann vassaye.
Shabad guru bhavsagar tareeye it ut eko jaaney.
Chinh varan nahi chhaaya maya Nanak shabad pachhaaney. 59.

सु सबद को निरँतर वास अलखँ जह देखां तह सोई।।
पवन का वासा सुँन निवासा अकल कला धर सोई।।
नदर करे सबद घट मह वसै विचों भरम गवाए।।
तन मन निरमल निरमल बाणी नामो नाम मन वसाए।।
सबद गुर भवसागर तरीए इत उत एको जाणै।।
चिहन वरन नही छाया माया नानक सबद पछाणै।। 59।।

Answer: "Naam flows continuously; wherever you look you can see it.
Like the air residing in *shunya*, ever-present and all-pervading.
With the Divine Grace it enters your heart when you get rid of doubt.
Just cleanse your body and mind with the Guru's word to welcome it in your heart
Let Naam be your guru and cross the ocean by knowing the One everywhere.
Recognise Naam which has no form or symbol, no illusion or shadow."

ਤ੍ਰੈਸਤ ਅੰਗੁਲ ਵਾਈ ਅਉਧੂ ਸੁੰਨ ਸਚੁ ਆਹਾਰੋ।।
ਗੁਰਮੁਖਿ ਬੋਲੈ ਤਤੁ ਬਿਰੋਲੈ ਚੀਨੈ ਅਲਖ ਅਪਾਰੋ।।
ਤ੍ਰੈਗੁਣ ਮੇਟੈ ਸਬਦੁ ਵਸਾਏ ਤਾ ਮਨਿ ਚੂਕੈ ਅਹੰਕਾਰੋ।।
ਅੰਤਰਿ ਬਾਹਰਿ ਏਕੋ ਜਾਣੈ ਤਾ ਹਰਿ ਨਾਮਿ ਲਗੈ ਪਿਆਰੋ।।
ਸੁਖਮਨਾ ਇੜਾ ਪਿੰਗੁਲਾ[7] ਬੂਝੈ ਜਾ ਆਪੇ ਅਲਖ ਲਖਾਏ।।
ਨਾਨਕ ਤਿਹੁ ਤੇ ਊਪਰਿ ਸਾਚਾ ਸਤਿਗੁਰ ਸਬਦਿ ਸਮਾਏ।।੬੦।।

Traisat angul vaayee Avdhu sunn sach aahaaro.
Gurmukh boley tatt biroley cheeney alakh apaaro.
Traigunn metey shabad vasaaye ta mann chookey ahankaaro.
Antar bahar eko jaaney ta Hari naam lagey pyaaro.
Sukhmana irha pingala boojhey ja aapey alakh lakhaaye.
Nanak tih te oopar sacha satgur shabad samaaye. 60.

त्रैसत अँगुल वाई अवधू सुँन सच आहारो।।
गुरमुख बोलै तत बिरोलै चीनै अलख अपारो।।
त्रैगुण मेटे सबद वसाए ता मन चूकै अहँकारो।।
अँतर बाहर एको जाणै ता हरि नाम लगै पिआरो।।
सुखमना इड़ा पिंगला बूझै जा आपे अलख लखाए।।
नानक तिह ते ऊपर साचा सतगुर सबद समाए।। 60।।

Answer continued: "Let me tell you, O Avdhu! that the support of breath is Naam.
Following the Guru's advice, the Gurmukh digs deep into his heart and finds the invisible.
He subdues the three attitudes, hosts the Word in his heart and destroys the ego.
When you see the One in and out then your heart wells up with love and overflows with it.
When the invisible becomes visible you can see it even in the three channels of your body.
The True One is above these methods of the yogis; you just get merged in it."

ਮਨ ਕਾ ਜੀਉ ਪਵਨੁ ਕਥੀਅਲੇ ਪਵਨੁ ਕਹਾ ਰਸੁ ਖਾਈ॥
ਗਿਆਨ ਕੀ ਮੁਦ੍ਰਾ ਕਵਨ ਅਉਧੂ ਸਿਧ ਕੀ ਕਵਨ ਕਮਾਈ॥
ਬਿਨੁ ਸਬਦੈ ਰਸੁ ਨ ਆਵੈ ਅਉਧੂ ਹਉਮੈ ਪਿਆਸ ਨ ਜਾਈ॥
ਸਬਦਿ ਰਤੇ ਅੰਮ੍ਰਿਤ ਰਸੁ ਪਾਇਆ ਸਾਚੇ ਰਹੇ ਅਘਾਈ॥
ਕਵਨ ਬੁਧਿ ਜਿਤੁ ਅਸਥਿਰੁ ਰਹੀਐ ਕਿਤੁ ਭੋਜਨਿ ਤ੍ਰਿਪਤਾਸੈ॥
ਨਾਨਕ ਦੁਖੁ ਸੁਖੁ ਸਮ ਕਰਿ ਜਾਪੈ ਸਤਿਗੁਰ ਤੇ ਕਾਲੁ ਨ ਗ੍ਰਾਸੈ॥੬੧॥

Mann ka jio pavan kathialey pavan kaha ras khaayee.
Gian ki mudra kavan kathialey Avdhu sidh ki kavan kamaayee.
Bin shabadey ras na aavey Avdhu haumei pyas na jaayee.
Shabad ratey amrit ras paya saachey rahey aghaayee.
Kavan budh jit asthir raheeye kit bhojan triptaasey.
Nanak dukh sukh sam kar jaapey satgur te kaal na graasey. 61.

मन का जीउ पवन कथीअले पवन कहा रस खाई।।
गिआन की मुद्रा कवन अवधू सिध की कवन कमाई।।
बिन सबदै रस न आवै अवधू हउमै पिआस न जाई।।
सबद रते अँमृत रस पाया साचे रहे अघाई।।
कवन बुध जित असथिर रहीए कित भोजन तृपतासै।।
नानक दुख सुख सम कर जापै सतगुर ते काल न ग्रासै।। 61।।

Question: "Air is said to be the life of the mind, but what does this air feed on?
What is the right posture of the yogi? What is the method of the siddha?"

Answer: "Naam is the alchemy to stablise the breath and to quench the thirst of the ego.
Coloured in Naam, you taste the nectar that grounds you in the all-pervasive divinity."

Question: "What is the method to be still? What is the food that will satisfy?"

Answer: "It is the greed of joys and the fear of sorrows that leads you astray.
Therefore, treat joys and sorrows equally; then there is no death or the fear of it.

ਰੰਗਿ ਨ ਰਾਤਾ ਰਸਿ ਨਹੀ ਮਾਤਾ॥
ਬਿਨੁ ਗੁਰ ਸਬਦੈ ਜਲਿ ਬਲਿ ਤਾਤਾ॥
ਬਿੰਦੁ ਨ ਰਾਖਿਆ ਸਬਦੁ ਨ ਭਾਖਿਆ॥
ਪਵਨੁ ਨ ਸਾਧਿਆ ਸਚੁ ਨ ਆਰਾਧਿਆ॥
ਅਕਥ ਕਥਾ ਲੇ ਸਮ ਕਰਿ ਰਹੈ॥
ਤਉ ਨਾਨਕ ਆਤਮ ਰਾਮ ਕਉ ਲਹੈ॥੬੨॥

Rang na raata ras nahi maata.
Bin gur shabadey jal bal taata.
Bind na raakhya shabad na bhaakhya.
Pavan na sadhya sach na aaradhya.
Akath katha ley sam kar rahey.
Tau Nanak atam Ram ko lahey. 62.

रँग न राता रस नही माता।।
बिन गुर सबदै जल बल ताता।।
बिंद न राखिया सबद न भाखिया।।
पवन न साधिया सच न आराधिया।।
अकथ कथा ले सम कर रहै।।
तौ नानक आतम राम को लहै।। 62।।

Without having tasted love or without being intoxicated with it,
And, without the Guru's word, you suffer as though you are on fire.
You are not a celebate if you have not let Naam resound in your body.
You have no control on your breath if you have not remembered Naam continuously.
If you understand the One that is beyond description and treat pain and pleasure equally,
Then you have arrived at the truth and you remain immersed in the all-pervading divinity.

ਗੁਰ ਪਰਸਾਦੀ ਰੰਗੇ ਰਾਤਾ॥
ਅੰਮ੍ਰਿਤੁ ਪੀਆ ਸਾਚੇ ਮਾਤਾ॥
ਗੁਰ ਵੀਚਾਰੀ ਅਗਨਿ ਨਿਵਾਰੀ॥
ਅਪਿਉ ਪੀਓ ਆਤਮ ਸੁਖੁ ਧਾਰੀ॥
ਸਚੁ ਅਰਾਧਿਆ ਗੁਰਮੁਖਿ ਤਰੁ ਤਾਰੀ॥
ਨਾਨਕ ਬੂਝੈ ਕੋ ਵੀਚਾਰੀ॥੬੩॥

Gur prasadi rangey rata.
Amrit piya saachey mata.
Gur veechaari agan nivaari.
Apiyo piyo atam sukh dhaari.
Sach araadhya gurmukh tar taari.
Nanak boojhey ko veechaari. 63.

गुर परसादी रँगे राता।।
अँमृत पीआ साचे माता।।
गुर वीचारी अगन निवारी।।
अपिउ पीओ आतम सुख धारी।।
सच अराधिया गुरमुख तर तारी।।
नानक बूझै को वीचारी।। 63।।

You can be dyed in divine shades only through the Guru's grace.
Then you are truly intoxicated with the Divine and become immortal.
The thought and remembrance of the Guru cools the fire within.
Then you have drunk the nectar and found peace within.
Remembering the Guru the *gurmukh* finds himself free of bondage.
There are very few rare individuals who chance upon this truth."

ਇਹੁ ਮਨੁ ਮੈਗਲੁ ਕਹਾ ਬਸੀਅਲੇ ਕਹਾ ਬਸੈ ਇਹੁ ਪਵਨਾ॥

ਕਹਾ ਬਸੈ ਸੁ ਸਬਦੁ ਅਉਧੂ ਤਾ ਕਉ ਚੂਕੈ ਮਨ ਕਾ ਭਵਨਾ॥

ਨਦਰਿ ਕਰੇ ਤਾ ਸਤਿਗੁਰੁ ਮੇਲੇ ਤਾ ਨਿਜ ਘਰਿ ਵਾਸਾ ਇਹੁ ਮਨੁ ਪਾਏ॥

ਆਪੈ ਆਪੁ ਖਾਇ ਤਾ ਨਿਰਮਲੁ ਹੋਵੈ ਧਾਵਤੁ ਵਰਜਿ ਰਹਾਏ॥

ਕਿਉ ਮੂਲੁ ਪਛਾਣੈ ਆਤਮੁ ਜਾਣੈ ਕਿਉ ਸਸਿ ਘਰਿ ਸੂਰੁ ਸਮਾਵੈ॥

ਗੁਰਮੁਖਿ ਹਉਮੈ ਵਿਚਹੁ ਖੋਵੈ ਤਉ ਨਾਨਕ ਸਹਜਿ ਸਮਾਵੈ॥੬੪॥

Eh mann maigal kaha baseealey kaha basey eh pavana.

Kaha basey su shabad Avdhu ta ko chookey mann ka bhavana.

Nadar karey ta satgur meley ta nij ghar vasa eh mann paaye.

Aapey aap khaye ta nirmal hovey dhavat varaj rahaaye.

Kyu mool pachhaney atam jaaney kyu sas ghar soor samavey.

Gurmukh haumei vichoh khovey tau Nanak sahaj samavey. 64.

इह मन मैगल कहा बसीअले कहा बसै इह पवना।।
कहा बसै सु सबद अवधू ता को चूकै मन का भवना।।
नदर करे ता सतगुर मेले ता निज घर वासा इह मन पाए।।
आपै आप खाए ता निरमल होवै धावत वरज रहाए।।
क्यों मूल पछाणै आतम जाणै क्यों ससि घर सूर समावै।।
गुरमुख हउमै विचों खोवै तौ नानक सहज समावै।। 64।।

Question: "Where does this huge elephant (mind) live? And where does the breath reside? And where does the Naam reside by which the mind's wanderings end?"

Answer: "With the compassionate Guru's grace the mind finds its home within itself By destroying the ego, the pure consciousness checks the wandering of the mind."

Question: "How to recognise the real? How to illumine the cold and dark moon?"
Answer: "The only way is to kill the ego, then you dissolve in the whole effortlessly.

ਇਹੁ ਮਨੁ ਨਿਹਚਲੁ ਹਿਰਦੈ ਵਸੀਅਲੇ ਗੁਰਮੁਖਿ ਮੂਲੁ ਪਛਾਣਿ ਰਹੈ॥
ਨਾਭਿ ਪਵਨੁ ਘਰਿ ਆਸਣਿ ਬੈਸੈ ਗੁਰਮੁਖਿ ਖੋਜਤ ਤਤੁ ਲਹੈ॥
ਸੁ ਸਬਦੁ ਨਿਰੰਤਰਿ ਨਿਜ ਘਰਿ ਆਛੈ ਤ੍ਰਿਭਵਣ ਜੋਤਿ ਸੁ ਸਬਦਿ ਲਹੈ॥
ਖਾਵੈ ਦੂਖ ਭੂਖ ਸਾਚੇ ਕੀ ਸਾਚੇ ਹੀ ਤ੍ਰਿਪਤਾਸਿ ਰਹੈ॥
ਅਨਹਦ ਬਾਣੀ ਗੁਰਮੁਖਿ ਜਾਣੀ ਬਿਰਲੋ ਕੋ ਅਰਥਾਵੈ॥
ਨਾਨਕ ਆਖੈ ਸਚੁ ਸੁਭਾਖੈ ਸਚਿ ਰਪੈ ਰੰਗੁ ਕਬਹੂ ਨ ਜਾਵੈ॥੬੫॥

Eh mann nehchal hirday vaseealey gurmukh mool pachhan rahey.
Naabh pavan ghar aasan baisey gurmukh khojat tatt rahey.
Su shabad nirantar nij ghar aachhey tribhavan jot su shabad lahey.
Khaavey dookh bhookh saachey ki saachey hi triptaas rahey.
Anhad bani gurmukh jaani birla ko arthaavey.
Nanak aakhey sach subhaakhey sach rapey rang kabhoo na jaavey. 65.

इह मन निहचल हिरदै वसीअले गुरमुख मूल पछाण रहै।।
नाभ पवन घर आसण बैसै गुरमुख खोजत तत लहै।।
सु सबद निरँतर निज घर आछै त्रिभवन जोत सु सबद लहै।।
खावै दूख भूख साचे की साचे ही तृपतास रहै।।
अनहद बाणी गुरमुख जाणी बिरले को अरथावै।।
नानक आखै सच सुभाखै सच रपै रँग कबहू न जावै।। 65।।

Grounded in his consciousness the *gurmukh* finds the truth.
Sitting still and breathing from the navel, the *gurmukh* finds the essence of reality.
When Naam resounds in his heart, the *gurmukh* sees the light that illumines the three worlds.
Having become one with the Divine, the *gurmukh* has no desire left of his own.
The *gurmukh* remains immersed in the unstruck sound of Naam. Very few can see this.
Then whatever he says is the truth for he is coloured in the indelible divine colours."

ਜਾ ਇਹੁ ਹਿਰਦਾ ਦੇਹ ਨ ਹੋਤੀ ਤਉ ਮਨੁ ਕੈਠੈ ਰਹਤਾ॥
ਨਾਭਿ ਕਮਲ ਅਸਥੰਭ ਨ ਹੋਤੋ ਤਾ ਪਵਨੁ ਕਵਨ ਘਰਿ ਸਹਤਾ॥
ਰੂਪੁ ਨ ਹੋਤੋ ਰੇਖ ਨ ਕਾਈ ਤਾ ਸਬਦਿ ਕਹਾ ਲਿਵ ਲਾਈ॥
ਰਕਤੁ ਬਿੰਦ ਕੀ ਮੜੀ ਨ ਹੋਤੀ ਮਿਤਿ ਕੀਮਤਿ ਨਹੀ ਪਾਈ॥
ਵਰਨੁ ਭੇਖੁ ਅਸਰੂਪੁ ਨ ਜਾਪੀ ਕਿਉ ਕਰਿ ਜਾਪਸਿ ਸਾਚਾ॥
ਨਾਨਕ ਨਾਮਿ ਰਤੇ ਬੈਰਾਗੀ ਇਬ ਤਬ ਸਾਚੋ ਸਾਚਾ॥੬੬॥

Ja eh hirda deh na hoti tau mann kaithey rahta.
Naabh kamal asthambh na hoto ta pavan kavan ghar sahta.
Roop na hoto rekh na kaayee ta shabad kaha liv laayee.
Rakat bind ki marhi na hoti mitt keemat nahi paayee.
Varan bhekh asaroop na jaapi kyu kar jaapas saacha.
Nanak naam ratey bairagi ib tab saacho saacha. 66.

जा इह हिरदा देह न होती तौ मन कैठै रहता।।
नाभि कमल असथँभ न होतो ता पवन कवन घर सहता।।
रूप न होतो रेख न काई ता सबद कहा लिव लाई।।
रकत बिंद की मड़ी न होती मित कीमत नही पाई।।
वरन भेख असरूप न जापी क्यों कर जापस साचा।।
नानक नाम रते बैरागी इब तब साचो साचा।। 66।।

Question: "When the body and heart did not exist, where did the mind reside?
When there was no lotus (navel), where did the breath come from?
When there was no form or shape, then how could one immerse in the Word?
With no body formed of egg and sperm, how could one know the value of the Divine?
With no signs or symbols and no form, how could one see the Divine?"

Answer: "By loving Naam you can see the Divine all the time and everywhere.

ਹਿਰਦਾ ਦੇਹ ਨ ਹੋਤੀ ਅਉਧੂ ਤਉ ਮਨੁ ਸੁੰਨਿ ਰਹੈ ਬੈਰਾਗੀ॥
ਨਾਭਿ ਕਮਲੁ ਅਸਥੰਭ ਨ ਹੋਤੋ ਤਾ ਨਿਜ ਘਰਿ ਬਸਤਉ ਪਵਨੁ ਅਨਰਾਗੀ॥
ਰੂਪੁ ਨ ਰੇਖਿਆ ਜਾਤਿ ਨ ਹੋਤੀ ਤਉ ਅਕੁਲੀਣਿ ਰਹਤਉ ਸਬਦੁ ਸੁ ਸਾਰੁ॥
ਗਉਨੁ ਗਗਨੁ ਜਬ ਤਬਹਿ ਹੋਤਉ ਤ੍ਰਿਭਵਣ ਜੋਤਿ ਆਪੇ ਨਿਰੰਕਾਰੁ॥
ਵਰਨੁ ਭੇਖੁ ਅਸਰੂਪੁ ਸੁ ਏਕੋ ਏਕੋ ਸਬਦੁ ਵਿਡਾਣੀ॥
ਸਾਚ ਬਿਨਾ ਸੂਚਾ ਕੋ ਨਾਹੀ ਨਾਨਕ ਅਕਥ ਕਹਾਣੀ॥੬੭॥

Hirda deh na hoti Avdhu tau mann sunn rahey bairagi.
Naabh kamal asathambh na hoto tau nij ghar bastoh pavan anragi.
Roop na rekhya jaat na hoti tau akuleen rahto shabad su saar.
Gaun gagan jab tabey hotoh tribhavan jot aapey nirankaar.
Varan bhekh asaroop su eko eko shabad vidaani.
Saach bina soocha ko naahi Nanak akath kahaani. 67.

हिरदा देह न होती अवधू तौ मन सुँन रहै बैरागी।।
नाभि कमल असथँभ न होतो ता निज घर बसतो पवन अनरागी।।
रूप न रेखिआ जात न होती तौ अकुलीण रहतो सबद सु सार।।
गौन गगन जब तबह होतो त्रिभवन जोत आपे निरँकार।।
वरन भेख असरूप सु एको एको सबद विडाणी।।
साच बिना सूचा को नाही नानक अकथ कहाणी।। 67।।

When there was no heart or body, the mind resided in the formless Divine.
When there was no support of navel the breath remained in its source drowned in love.
When there was no shape or form the Word remained as an undistinct part of the whole.
When the earth or sky did not exist the light of the formless Divine filled the three worlds.
And, wonder of wonders, the hidden forms and colours have come to light!
The basic truth is that there is nothing in this world that is not divine and pure."

ਕਿਤੁ ਬਿਧਿ ਜਗੁ ਉਪਜੈ ਪੁਰਖਾ ਕਿਤੁ ਬਿਧਿ ਦੁਖਿ ਬਿਨਸਿ ਜਾਈ॥
ਹਉਮੈ ਵਿਚਿ ਜਗੁ ਉਪਜੈ ਪੁਰਖਾ ਨਾਮਿ ਵਿਸਰਿਐ ਦੁਖੁ ਪਾਈ॥
ਗੁਰਮੁਖਿ ਹੋਵੈ ਸੁ ਗਿਆਨੁ ਤਤੁ ਬੀਚਾਰੈ ਹਉਮੈ ਸਬਦਿ ਜਲਾਏ॥
ਤਨੁ ਮਨੁ ਨਿਰਮਲੁ ਨਿਰਮਲ ਬਾਣੀ ਸਾਚੈ ਰਹੈ ਸਮਾਏ॥
ਨਾਮੇ ਨਾਮਿ ਰਹੈ ਬੈਰਾਗੀ ਸਾਚੁ ਰਖਿਆ ਉਰਿ ਧਾਰੇ॥
ਨਾਨਕ ਬਿਨੁ ਨਾਵੈ ਜੋਗੁ ਕਦੇ ਨ ਹੋਵੈ ਦੇਖਹੁ ਰਿਦੈ ਬੀਚਾਰੇ॥੬੮॥

Kit bidh jag upajey purkha kit bidh dukh binas jaayee.
Haumei vich jag upajey purkha naam visareeye dukh paayee.
Gurmukh hovey so gyan tatt beechaarey haumei shabad jalaaye.
Tann mann nirmal nirmal baani saachey rahey samaaye.
Naamey naam rahey bairagi saach rakhya ur dhaarey.
Nanak bin naavey jog kadey na hovey dekho ridey beechaarey. 68.

कित बिधि जग उपजै पुरखा कित बिधि दुख बिनस जाई।।
हउमै विच जग उपजै पुरखा नाम विसरीए दुख पाई।।
गुरमुख होवै सु गिआन तत बीचारे हउमै सबद जलाए।।
तन मन निरमल निरमल बाणी साचै रहै समाए।।
नामे नाम रहै बैरागी साच रखिआ उर धारे।।
नानक बिन नावै जोग कदे न होवै देखो रिदै बीचारे।। 68।।

Question: "How was the world formed? What disaster will end it?"

Answer: "This visible world was born out of ego. Forgetting Naam it suffers and perishes.
The *gurmukh* aligns himself with true wisdom and lets Naam destroy his ego.
Thus he purifies his body and mind and remains immersed in the True One.
He makes his heart the abode of Naam and Naam remains constant in it.
Look within and know that without Naam no yoga is possible.

ਗੁਰਮੁਖਿ ਸਾਚੁ ਸਬਦੁ ਬੀਚਾਰੈ ਕੋਇ॥
ਗੁਰਮੁਖਿ ਸਚੁ ਬਾਣੀ ਪਰਗਟੁ ਹੋਇ॥
ਗੁਰਮੁਖਿ ਮਨੁ ਭੀਜੈ ਵਿਰਲਾ ਬੂਝੈ ਕੋਇ॥
ਗੁਰਮੁਖਿ ਨਿਜ ਘਰਿ ਵਾਸਾ ਹੋਇ॥
ਗੁਰਮੁਖਿ ਜੋਗੀ ਜੁਗਤਿ ਪਛਾਣੈ॥
ਗੁਰਮੁਖਿ ਨਾਨਕ ਏਕੋ ਜਾਣੈ॥੬੯॥

Gurmukh saach shabad beechaarey koye.
Gurmukh sach baani pargat hoye.
Gurmukh mann bheejey virla boojhey koye.
Gurmukh nij ghar vaasa hoye.
Gurmukh jogi jugat pachhaaney.
Gurmukh Nanak eko jaaney. 69.

गुरमुख साच सबद बीचारे कोए।।
गुरमुख सच बाणी परगट होए।।
गुरमुख मन भीजै विरला बूझै कोए।।
गुरमुख निज घर वासा होए।।
गुरमुख जोगी जुगत पछाणै।।
गुरमुख नानक एको जाणै।। 69।।

The *gurmukh* is the one who reflects on Naam.
The *gurmukh* understands the essence of *gurbani.*
The *gurmukh* is drenched in love although very few can see it.
The *gurmukh* remains grounded in his consciousness.
The *gurmukh* is the true yogi who knows the *yukti* (method) of attainment.
The *gurmukh* sees the One in everyone and everything.

ਬਿਨੁ ਸਤਿਗੁਰ ਸੇਵੇ ਜੋਗੁ ਨ ਹੋਈ॥
ਬਿਨੁ ਸਤਿਗੁਰ ਭੇਟੇ ਮੁਕਤਿ ਨ ਕੋਈ॥
ਬਿਨੁ ਸਤਿਗੁਰ ਭੇਟੇ ਨਾਮੁ ਪਾਇਆ ਨ ਜਾਇ॥
ਬਿਨੁ ਸਤਿਗੁਰ ਭੇਟੇ ਮਹਾ ਦੁਖੁ ਪਾਇ॥
ਬਿਨੁ ਸਤਿਗੁਰ ਭੇਟੇ ਮਹਾ ਗਰਬਿ ਗੁਬਾਰਿ॥
ਨਾਨਕ ਬਿਨੁ ਗੁਰ ਮੁਆ ਜਨਮੁ ਹਾਰਿ॥੭੦॥

Bin satgur sevey jog na hoyee.
Bin satgur bhetey mukat na koyee.
Bin satgur bhetey naam paya na jaye.
Bin satgur bhetey maha dukh paye.
Bin satgur bhetey maha garab gubaar.
Nanak bin gur muaa janam haar. 70.

बिन सतगुर सेवे जोग न होई।।
बिन सतगुर भेटे मुकत न कोई।।
बिन सतगुर भेटे नाम पाया न जाए।।
बिन सतगुर भेटे महा दुख पाए।।
बिन सतगुर भेटे महा गरब गुबार।।
नानक बिन गुर मुआ जनम हार।। 70।।

You cannot be perfect in yoga without abiding by the Guru's advice.
You cannot be liberated without meeting the Guru.
You cannot obtain Naam without meeting the Guru.
You are likely to suffer in pain without meeting the Guru.
You remain imprisoned in the darkness of ego without the Guru.
You remain bound in the cycle of birth and death without the Guru.

ਗੁਰਮੁਖਿ ਮਨੁ ਜੀਤਾ ਹਉਮੈ ਮਾਰਿ॥
ਗੁਰਮੁਖਿ ਸਾਚੁ ਰਖਿਆ ਉਰ ਧਾਰਿ॥
ਗੁਰਮੁਖਿ ਜਗੁ ਜੀਤਾ ਜਮਕਾਲੁ ਮਾਰਿ ਬਿਦਾਰਿ॥
ਗੁਰਮੁਖਿ ਦਰਗਹ ਨ ਆਵੈ ਹਾਰਿ॥
ਗੁਰਮੁਖਿ ਮੇਲਿ ਮਿਲਾਏ ਸੁ ਜਾਣੈ॥
ਨਾਨਕ ਗੁਰਮੁਖਿ ਸਬਦਿ ਪਛਾਣੈ॥੭੧॥

Gurmukh mann jeeta haumei maar.
Gurmukh saach rakhya ur dhaar.
Gurmuk jag jeeta jamkaal maar bidaar.
Gurmukh dargah na aavey haar.
Gurmukh meil milaaye so jaaney.
Nanak gurmukh shabad pachhaaney. 71.

गुरमुख मन जीता हउमै मार।।
गुरमुख साच रखिआ उर धार।।
गुरमुख जग जीता जमकाल मार बिदार।।
गुरमुख दरगह न आवै हार।।
गुरमुख मेल मिलाए सु जाणै।।
नानक गुरमुख सबद पछाणै।। 71।।

The *gurmukh* conquers his mind by subduing his ego.
The *gurmukh* makes room for Naam in his heart.
The *gurmukh* conquers death and becomes free from this mortal world.
The *gurmukh* will not fail when judged in the Divine Court.
The *gurmukh* is like a drop of water that falls into the ocean and becomes one with it.
The *gurmukh* realises the true meaning of Naam.

ਸਬਦੈ ਕਾ ਨਿਬੇੜਾ ਸੁਣਿ ਤੂ ਅਉਧੂ ਬਿਨੁ ਨਾਵੈ ਜੋਗੁ ਨ ਹੋਈ॥
ਨਾਮੇ ਰਾਤੇ ਅਨਦਿਨੁ ਮਾਤੇ ਨਾਮੈ ਤੇ ਸੁਖੁ ਹੋਈ॥
ਨਾਮੈ ਹੀ ਤੇ ਸਭੁ ਪਰਗਟੁ ਹੋਵੈ ਨਾਮੇ ਸੋਝੀ ਪਾਈ॥
ਬਿਨੁ ਨਾਵੈ ਭੇਖ ਕਰਹਿ ਬਹੁਤੇਰੇ ਸਚੈ ਆਪਿ ਖੁਆਈ॥
ਸਤਿਗੁਰ ਤੇ ਨਾਮੁ ਪਾਈਐ ਅਉਧੂ ਜੋਗ ਜੁਗਤਿ ਤਾ ਹੋਈ॥
ਕਰਿ ਬੀਚਾਰੁ ਮਨਿ ਦੇਖਹੁ ਨਾਨਕ ਬਿਨੁ ਨਾਵੈ ਮੁਕਤਿ ਨ ਹੋਈ॥੭੨॥

Shabadey ka nibera sunn tu Avdhu bin naavey jog na hoyee.
Naamey raatey andin maatey naamey te sukh hoyee.
Naamey hi te sabh pargat hovey naamey sojhi paayee.
Bin naavey bhekh karey bahutere sachey aap khuaayee.
Satgur te naam payeeye Avdhu jog jugat ta hoyee.
Kar bichaar mann dekho Nanak bin naavey mukat na hoyee. 72.

सबदै का निबेड़ा सुन तू अवधू बिन नावै जोग न होई।।
नामे राते अनदिन माते नामै ते सुख होई।।
नामै ही ते सभ परगट होवै नामे सोझी पाई।।
बिन नावै भेख करे बहुतेरे सचै आप खुआई।।
सतगुर ते नाम पाईए अवधू जोग जुगत ता होई।।
कर बीचार मन देखो नानक बिन नावै मुकत न होई।। 72।।

O Yogi! The sum total of this dialogue is Naam. No yoga is possible without Naam.
You can gain all the fruits of Naam if you remain immersed in it.
It is Naam that reveals all secrets and Naam gives realisation.
Without Naam all else is only pretence, leading you astray (away from the Truth).
O Yogi, seek Naam from the true Guru and your yoga is complete.
Think about it honestly, there is no freedom without Naam.

ਤੇਰੀ ਗਤਿ ਮਿਤਿ ਤੂ ਹੈ ਜਾਣਹਿ ਕਿਆ ਕੋ ਆਖਿ ਵਖਾਣੈ॥
ਤੂ ਆਪੇ ਗੁਪਤਾ ਆਪੇ ਪਰਗਟੁ ਆਪੇ ਸਭਿ ਰੰਗ ਮਾਣੈ॥
ਸਾਧਿਕ ਸਿਧ ਗੁਰੂ ਬਹੁ ਚੇਲੇ ਖੋਜਤ ਫਿਰਹਿ ਫੁਰਮਾਣੈ॥
ਮਾਗਹਿ ਨਾਮੁ ਪਾਇ ਇਹ ਭਿਖਿਆ ਤੇਰੇ ਦਰਸਨ ਕਉ ਕੁਰਬਾਣੈ॥
ਅਬਿਨਾਸੀ ਪ੍ਰਭਿ ਖੇਲੁ ਰਚਾਇਆ ਗੁਰਮੁਖਿ ਸੋਝੀ ਹੋਈ॥
ਨਾਨਕ ਸਭਿ ਜੁਗ ਆਪੇ ਵਰਤੈ ਦੂਜਾ ਅਵਰੁ ਨ ਕੋਈ॥੭੩॥ ੧॥

Teri gat mit tu hai jaaney kya ko aakh vakhaaney.
Tu aapey gupta aapey pargat aapey sabh rang maaney.
Saadhik sidh gur bahu cheley khojat firey furmaaney.
Maangey naam paaye eh bhikhya tere darshan ko kurbaaney.
Abinaasi prabh khel rachaaya gurmukh sojhi hoyee.
Nanak sabh jug aapey vartey duja avar na koyee. 73.

तेरी गत मित तू है जाणै कया को आख वखाणै।।
तू आपे गुपता आपे परगट आपे सभ रँग माणै।।
साधिक सिध गुर बहु चेले खोजत फिरे फुरमाणै।।
मांगे नाम पाए इह भिखिआ तेरे दरसन को कुरबाणै।।
अबिनासी प्रभ खेल रचाया गुरमुख सोझी होई।।
नानक सभ जुग आपे वरतै दूजा अवर न कोई।। 73।। 1।।

You alone know your secrets; what can anyone say about it.
You are the hidden and the revealed and you enjoy everything.
The seekers and siddhas are many who are in search of the truth.
They seek Naam and find it with your blessings; I surrender to thee.
This play is staged by the Immortal Being; the *gurmukh* gets a glimpse of it.
Ultimately, it is the One that exists in all the ages; there is no other that exists."

Appendix

1. Sahaj

Sahaj is the state of being that is considered as the ultimate state in *Gurbani. Sahaj* means being in your natural state. It means living life as it comes. It means doing your duties but without being the doer. *Sahaj* means effortless effort; the only effort we need to make is to remove the dust of conditioning which includes our thoughts, beliefs, likes, dislikes, biases, prejudices etc from the clean slate that we were in in our original form.

Gurbani refers to *sahaj* as the fourth state of being above the three states of *tamas, rajas* and *sattva. Tamas* is the lowest of the three. It is a force which promotes darkness, death, destruction, ignorance, inertia and resistance. It is the lowest, heaviest, slowest, and most dull (for example, a stone or a lump of earth). It is devoid of the energy of the *rajas* and the brightness of *sattva. Rajas* is action-driven. It is never satisfied and never at rest. *Rajasic* people strive for more and more in position or possessions. They display jealousy, cruelty, selfishness and arrogance. *Sattvic* people are naturally intelligent, instinctively clear-headed, calm, contented, considerate and sensitive. *Sattva* is a mind type that is open and positive, always willing to learn, eager to help and generally happy.

Sahaj is the state of being when the mind rests in its conscious state. Having become absolutely calm and peaceful, it is grounded in its most natural form. In this state you live a natural life, taking care of your basic needs without attaching emotions to them. You live as life comes to you from one moment to another without thinking of the past and dreaming about the future, for the past is dead and gone and irreversible, and the future is not yet, may or may not happen, and absolutely unpredictable.

In the state of *sahaj* when you get rid of all the external frills and trappings of dreams and desires of the future and grudges and grievances of the past, you live in the present moment. In this moment alone you are truly alive. You vibrate with life and overflow with love.

The kind of life each one of us has to live in society is almost all pretence. It is the need of the society that we pretend to be someone other than our self. Suppose, someone says something nasty to you, your instinctive response might be to slap the person—but you are not supposed to do that. So, you repress your anger and pretend to be civil to the person whereas in reality you would have behaved otherwise. You may have succeeded in repressing your natural instinct but it does not disappear; it goes down into your unconscious mind and creates problems for you without your realising it. Thus, you get torn between what you really want to do and what you actually do. These are compulsions of living in society because you have to respect others' rights as much as you want to enjoy your rights. As long as we live in the world of men and women we have to abide by these norms. Even if we were to go to the forest, we would still have to live by some norms—which may be simpler—but are there all the same.

Then, what is the way out? How to come to the state of *sahaj* while living in this world? The answer is simple. Just become aware of it. Know that you are only abiding by the rules, and don't get attached to them. Don't identify yourself with the task you are performing. Just as you don't spare a second thought when you are driving on the left side of the road, go about doing your duty in the same detached manner. If you drive on the wrong side of the road, no God will come to punish you but you are likely to hit against something or someone and get hurt. Similarly, when you do good you feel good and the bad that you do to others makes you feel much worse. Here, rewards and punishments are inbuilt. These are all cash transactions. Whatever is, is here and now. There is no point brooding about the past or dreaming about the future. *Sahaj* is living the "now" moment. Sounds easy? But once you start practising it, you will realise how difficult it is; But, it is only difficult, not impossible. It would have been impossible if it was not your intrinsic nature. Then there would have been no way to impose it on you. But, the fact is that all the other things have been brought from the outside. All the memories and the dreams have come from the outside and covered your basic nature of *sahaj*. All you have to do is to remove these external obstructions.

And, the method to remove this burden is to look at it squarely in the eye–and it is gone. These dreams (desires) and memories exist because they are stored in the darkness of the unconscious mind. Bring them out in the open and they will vanish. They survive in the darkness; let them come in the light and they will disappear along with the darkness.

There is darkness inside which invites the three mind types to play their games without any hindrance. Each one of us has a combination of attributes of *tamas*, *rajas* and *sattva*. The difference is only in the balance. Some might have more *sattvic gunas* and the others might have more *rajasic* or *tamasic gunas*. The difference between them is only of degree and not of kind. We are bound by them and have become slaves to them. We have mistaken them to be our intrinsic nature. We allow them to dictate our thought, speech and action. We have allowed this darkness to not only exist in us but to grow to tremendous proportions. How? Why have we let these *gunas* take the reins in their hands?

We have let this darkness grow because we have never looked in.

All we need to do is to change the direction of the eyes, of our sense of sight. All our senses function outside. Our eyes look at things that are outside; our ears hear the sounds coming from outside; our nose smells outside things and so on. They are the doors and windows that connect us to the world. Now, doors and windows are two-way passages. The same door has 'pull' and 'push' written on it. The same door allows you to go in and go out. The difference is only in the direction. Exactly the same happens with our senses. They function outside. This is how Nature has made them, because they are our tools to connect with the world.

In order to change the direction we have to make an effort. The eyes are only the windows. It is you who looks through them. It is you who is right behind the eye looking outside. All you have to do is to take an about turn and direct the arrow of your vision inside. When you look within you are not just an observer but also the observed because you are looking at yourself. It is an arduous task and will require a tremendous amount of effort because you have to change the flow of the current. But, ultimately when you become the object of your observation you are in a state of *sahaj*. *Sahaj* is when the observer becomes the observed.

An arduous task indeed! Therefore you need to have immense patience and the capacity to wait indefinitely. The more you go in the harder it gets because even things which had been buried deep in the unconscious mind also start popping up. All thoughts, feelings, emotions, moods are from outside. They will pull you outwards with all their might. Therefore, you need to be patient and keep persevering. A loving and prayerful attitude will help. Just remain determined to watch everything, no matter what the distractions. Your attention will be distracted; take it in your stride. Come back to observing when you remember to do so. Keep at it, no matter what.

You don't need to do anything else. There is no need to go anywhere. All you need to do is watch everything. Become aware of everything. Become a witness. Become a *sakshi.* Don't let anything go by without looking at it. This is your prayer: Look at everything that life gives you! This is the state of *sahaj.*

Sahaj is looking at each moment as it comes. If it brings joy, look at it without being affected by it and without getting attached to it. If you get attached to it you will run away with it, you will get absorbed in it and you will go away from the moment and you will not be able to look at it. You can only see that which is at a distance from you. You have to learn the art of looking, which entails looking from a distance. You need to create a distance between you–the observer– and you–the observed.

Gurbani says this state of *sahaj* is the ultimate state of being which everyone covets. The pundits, priests, yogis and *siddhas* are all aiming to achieve this state, but often they go astray, because they try to change their demeanour in order to change their attitude. They make changes in their life style; they leave their homes and give up the world. In other words, they try to bring changes inside through external behaviour, which is putting the cart before the horse. The conduct that is imposed from the outside is only skin-deep. It cannot last long. Only when the transformation happens inside, will the outward demeanour change automatically. As long as you are wandering in the maze of these three *gunas*, you are in delusion; you will go on moving in circles and reach nowhere. *Sahaj* is only in the fourth state.

Gurbani insists on the need of a Guru who can help the seeker change his attitude. The Guru is the link between the seeker and the sought. The Guru is one who has walked the path and can show you the way. But, it is you who have to walk on it.

Gurbani talks about the apparent paradox that exists in *sahaj* as in everything else in Nature. Everything is so interconnected and inter-dependent that no one can give any explanation to prove their point. For example, no one can say whether the chick came first or the egg. No one can say with any amount of certainty whether the seed comes from the tree or the tree comes from the seed. They exist in a chain of cause and effect. Similarly, *Gurbani* says that *sahaj* is the ultimate state and yet you cannot even begin your spiritual journey without being in a state of *sahaj*. So, *sahaj* is the first step and also the last step. *Sahaj* is the means and the end. It is only when you are in a state of *sahaj*, in your natural state that you will be able to look at the moment; only then you will be able to listen to the Guru's Word; become loving and prayerful, become passive and patient to receive the divine blessings. It is only when you are in the state of *sahaj* that you will realise your true self, you will know who you are.

2. *Duniya Sagar*

This world is considered as an ocean of fire (*agan-sagar*) which is impossible to cross. It is what keeps us bound like prisoners and we strive in every possible way to break these chains and become free. From the moment we are born to the time of death, we are thrown from one event to another, from one direction to another; like a rudderless boat in the stormy sea. All religions describe this world as an ocean and give their own ways and means to cross over based on their own understanding and experience. *Gurbani* refers to it again and again. While it illucidates the perils of being bound in this world, it also suggests the remedy to break free.

This same world (*sansar*) is also called maya. Maya means illusion–that which appears to be but is not. There are two strong and diametrically opposite views on maya. The first group thinks all that is visible is illusory because it is short-lived, temporary, transient. You cannot rely on it, therefore, it should be shunned. The other group thinks that this world is all that is there, therefore, make the most of it. Why worry about things that are not visible, and give up on that which is there? The hold of maya is strong on both the groups. While one indulges in it and has become a slave to it, and feels imprisoned in its clutches, the other group is terrified by it and runs away from it. While they claim it is illusory yet they renounce it, which is a contradiction in itself and they remain bound to it nonetheless.

This world or maya is dangerous because it is deceptive. It appears to be beautiful and attractive; enchanting and captivating. But, it is like the bait to catch the fish. Just as the fish gets tempted by the food and comes for it only to get caught in the net, man is attrcted by the multi-splendoured world only to get caught in its prison. The only difference between the hedonists and the spiritualists is that while the prison of the hedonist is visible because it is made of iron and keeps you chained in it, the prison of the spiritualist is made of gold; it doesn't look like a prison because it promises freedom–but somewhere in the future. Freedom promised in the future is of no significance. If it is not here and now, it is of no use. A cage is a cage whether it is made of gold or iron. Fetters, though of gold are no less strong to bind. In fact, the fetters of gold are even more dangerous because they wear the garb of freedom.

The world is an illusion because of our interpretation of things. We never look at anything as it is; we always look at things through our tainted glasses, the glasses coloured by our deep-rooted conditioning. We are always passing judgements: this is good or this is bad; this is right or that is wrong. All these pre-conceived notions stand in our way and blur our vision. That is why we all live in our own worlds. We do not occupy the same world. We live in our own shells; each one of us carries our own world around us. There are as many worlds as there are individuals. And, it is this world made of conditioning and interpretation that is illusory. It has nothing to do with things as they are. The world is in fact neutral. It is our conditioning that makes it good or bad. And, that, is an illusion.

For example, you see a man on the road who is being chased by the police. Your first thought would be that he must be a thief. Now, without knowing anything about him, you have already passed a verdict on his character. Then, may be you had a closer look and found out that he belongs to a certain community. You, at once, feel scared of him. He might be a terrorist. Within minutes, you are quite sure that he is one. Yet, the fact remains that you know nothing about him. But, you have already condemned him. This is maya–the world of illusion.

The irony of it is that the illusory world of maya has become so powerful that it has hidden the real world. We have lost the ability to see things as they are. We look at them through the prism of our mind, which distorts everything. The mind is like a small keyhole and the world is the vast open sky. We look at it through the keyhole. No wonder we see only a tiny speck of it and we base our actions and reactions on what we see through the keyhole. We have no idea what the bigger picture is–but, according to our mind, we are pretty vocal about what should the picture be!

This maya has become overwhelming because of our identification with it. On its own, it is nothing better than a dream, which appears to be real but which disappears as soon as you wake up. This maya has become insurmountable because we have identified ourselves with what we see outside. We have aligned ourselves with the external which is transient, illusory and false.

All religions agree on the fact that this ocean is extremely difficult, if not impossible, to cross. Firstly, because of being in it, we are not even aware of the fact that we are caught. Then where is the question of breaking away ? Secondly, we are going round and round in it like a whirlpool. No wonder it is called *bhavsagar*. We are born, we live for a while and then we die to be reborn, re-live and re-die. This cycle of birth and death goes on and on. We have no idea when it began and when and if it will ever end. Thirdly, because this is the known pattern of life; it happens with everyone and we are no exception. We are not aware of any other way of life, so, we accept it unquestioningly. On the contrary, we question the veracity of the assertions of a few exceptional beings who have seen the light like Gautama Buddha, Jesus Christ, Guru Nanak and other such enlightened masters.

What is this world? How does it bind us? What is the way to break these chains and be free? This needs to be pondered on. What binds us? Can the trees, the mountains keep us captive? Do the sun, moon and stars hold us prisoners? No. Then, what is it that keeps us in bondage? We, ourselves are responsible for our bondage. It is our mind that has built this labyrinth of chains that seems to tighten the noose round our necks day and night. The mind is never satisfied; the more it gets the more it wants. The mind is a bottomless pit; whatever you put in it gets absorbed and it asks for more. It is led by the ego, and it serves the ego. The ego is jealous; it wants more than the others have. The ego is greedy; it has an unquenchable thirst for more and more. The ego is competitive; it wants to do better than everybody else. Basically, the ego keeps making demands and the mind rushes at full speed to meet those demands. There are desires, wishes, longings, aspirations galore. When one desire is fulfilled, ten others crop up in its place. When they are fulfilled hundred others come up involuntarily. There is not a moment's gap. The more you achieve the more you aspire. The truth is that we have become slaves to our minds. The mind keeps presenting problems and we spend all our energy in solving them. The mind keeps making demands and we keep bending over backwards to meet them. The mind flies on the wings of fantasy and we run after it, trying to keep pace with it. There is not a moment when the mind is at rest. And, we follow it helplessly, unable to put it in its proper place. The mind has become the master and we have become its slaves. This is the bondage that the religions speak of. This is the ocean of fire that has to be crossed–the ocean of desires and expectations!

The good news is that once the problem is understood and stated clearly, the solution is not difficult to find. We have all experienced in greater or smaller degrees that expectaions lead to frustration. The more you expect, the more frustrated you are. If expectation is one side of the coin, then frustration is the other side of the same coin. Desire and despair go hand in hand. They come in the same package.

The first thing for understanding is that the ocean of fire is not somewhere far away, in the future or after death. It is right here. You have gone through it many times when your desires have not been fulfilled, when things have happened against your wishes. All you need to do is to take a good look at the desires that keep cropping up in your mind. And, as soon as you see them for what they are, they will disappear. You have seen the full circle of many desires. You have seen a desire arise in your mind; you have worked hard to fulfill it; as soon as it is fulfilled you have lost interest in it; and, a new one has taken its place. If you have seen the whole thing from beginning to end, you will realise the futility of it. You will wonder at the stupidity of chasing desires, which is like little children chasing butterflies. We are all grown-up kids chasing our dreams. When you see the futility of it, it will drop automatically. This is the secret. Watch the desire arise and see it grow, but don't do anything. Just look at it. That is enough. It will not be able to stand in front of your gaze. It could grow only in the darkness of your unconsciousness. The moment you become conscious of it, it ceases to exist. Awareness is the key. Just focus your attention on it, be alert, and see it evaporating like dew drops in the morning sun.

3. Six Shastras

Sankhya, Nyaya, Vaishashika, Mimamsa, Yoga and Vedanta.

4. Spiritual Qualities of Five Elements

Sky = detachment

Fire = extinction of filth

Earth = patience

Water = cleanliness

Air = equality

5. Nine Treasures

Padam = gold, silver

Maha padam = perals, diamonds

Sankh = rich food and clothing

Makar = valour, mastery of martial arts

Kachhap = merchandise trade

Kund = gold/preciuos stones trade

Mukand = mastery of fine arts

Eighteen Spiritual Powers (*Siddhis*)

Anima = To take on another's form

Mahima = To enhance the body

Laghima = To contract the body

Garima = To become weighty

Prapati = To get whatever is desired

Prakamya = To know what is in the other's mind

Ishita = To dictate others as per your wishes

Vishita = To control everybody

Anuram = to have no thirst or hunger

Door shravan = To hear from far away

Door darshan = To see from far away

Manoveg = To travel at the speed of thought

Kaam roop = To acquire a desired form

Parkaye pravesh = To enter another's body

Swachhand mrityu = To die when you wish to

Sur krira = To rejoice in the company of gods

Sankalp siddhi = To achieve whatever you wish

Apratigat = To go wherever you want without any hindrance

6. *Gurmukh* vs *Manmukh*

Gurmukh literally means one who has his face towards the Guru, and *manmukh* is one who has turned his back towards the Guru. It means that the *gurmukh* is ready to listen to the Guru and follow his advice, whereas the *manmukh* follows his own mind and is incapable of listening to the Guru. The *gurmukh* recognises that he knows nothing and looks up to the Guru to enlighten him and lead him. The *manmukh* thinks he knows everything because he has a fertile mind that is forever talking to him. The *gurmukh* realises that his mind is just like a window, a keyhole through which he cannot see the whole sky. The *manmukh* looks through the keyhole (mind) and thinks he has seen the whole sky. The *manmukh* acts according to the tiny picture he can see whereas the *gurmukh* places the Guru's word above his own limited understanding and allows the Guru to lead him. The Guru is the link between the *gurmukh* and the Divine. The Guru has seen the bigger picture and can guide the disciple if the latter would let him. The *gurmukh* allows it and benefits by it; the *manmukh* does not allow it and goes astray.

7. Ida, Pingla, Sukhmana

Ida, Pingala and *Sukhmana* (*sushumna*) are *nadis* (channels) in the body. They are astral tubes made up of astral matter that carry Pranic currents. They can be seen by the astral eyes only. They are not the nerves. According to yoga, there are 72,000 *nadis*. *Ida, Pingala* and *Sukhmana* are the important ones; *Sukhmana* being the most important of all.

There are two nerve-currents; one on the either side of the spinal column. The left one is called *Ida* and the right one is called *Pingala*. These are *nadis* or subtle tubes that carry Prana. The moon moves in the *Ida* and the sun in *Pingala*. *Ida* is cooling. *Pingala* is heating. *Ida* flows through the left nostril and *Pingala* through the right.

Sukhmana is the most important of all the nadis. Situated at the back of the tailbone, it is attached to the spinal column and extends to the *Brahmarandhra* of the head. It runs along the centre of the spinal cord.

Yoga is based on the purification of these nadis through pranayama.

₹ 100.00

Guru Nanak walked on this earth more than five hundred years ago. Wherever he set his foot has become a place of worship. Whatever he said rings true till date and is more relevant now than ever before. Whatever he did had immense depth and profound meaning in it. The stories that evolved around his divine presence are called *Janam Sakhis*.

The Singer Divine is a poetic rendering of stories from the life of Guru Nanak. These are stories retold in ballads. Each ballad describes an event and the steps of that event move dramatically forward. The language is simple but elegant. Once you pick up the book you can't put it down till you have finished reading it.

Satjit Wadva has retold the stories in an amazingly refreshing manner, retaining the pure and offering interpretations that appeal to the rational minds as much as to the devoted heart.

₹ 195.00

This is a story. It may not be factual but it is true. Let's leave it to the fools to fight and argue whether the Ka'aba actually moved or not. But the fact remains there's not the slighest space where God is not.

Guru Nanak, the singer, sang in tune with the song of nature. He sang of matters down-to-earth and truths deep and profound. He sang and Mardana played the rabaab. He sang and people flocked around. Men, women, children, animals and birds listened to him spellbound.